# BTRIPP BOOKS

## BOOK REVIEWS FROM

# 2014

### BY BRENDAN TRIPP

These reviews originally appeared on the
"BTRIPP'S BOOKS" book review blog:
http://btripp-books.livejournal.com/

Copyright © 2016 by Brendan Tripp

ISBN 978-1-57353-414-7

An Eschaton Book

http://www.EschatonBooks.com

Front cover photo courtesy Kenn W. Kiser via morguefile.com.
Back cover photo courtesy Sebastian Santana via morguefile.com.

# PREFACE

From 1993 through 2004, I ran the *first* manifestation of Eschaton Books (now in its third revival). Initially started as a vehicle to publish my poetry, it soon became evident that the market for poetry is vanishingly small, and in 1994 we "pivoted" into being a metaphysical press.

During this time, I was largely a one-man shop, doing everything from editorial to shipping, which was a huge time commitment, and I typically worked 14 hour days, 7 days a week to keep things moving. I bring up all this here because, despite having been a life-long avid reader, during this period I had precious little time for reading, and what reading I *did* get done was largely reviewing book submissions. However, I never stopped *buying* books, which began to stack up in prodigious "to be read" piles.

When Eschaton went out of business (in a not unusual *denouement* for a small press – we had a distributor who ended up never paying us, while selling through all our stock) in 2004, I found myself with a lot of reading to catch up on, and a need to keep my writing chops sharp. So, I began to pen little reviews of what I was reading through, and post those on the web.

As the years went by, this became "a thing" that I was doing, and, for a while, I was targeting a fairly aggressive goal of getting at least 72 non-fiction books read per year. By 2015, this had resulted in my having read and reviewed 700 books over that 12-year span.

In recent years (since the upswing in print-on-demand publishing), I have had *numerous* acquaintances suggest that I put out my reviews as books. I was, at first, rather hesitant on the concept (as, after all, the material was free to read on the web), but I eventually figured that if various people thought it was a good idea, I might as well give it a shot.

While I could have started at the beginning, with the reviews from 2004, I decided that those were less representtative of the whole, so opted to begin with the most recent ones. While having fewer reviews than most years (I pulled back from the 72-book target after 2012), this is the second of these collections, representing what I put up on my review site in 2014.

A note on my review "style": I do not write classic reviews, but more a telling of my personal interaction with a particular book. This means that I talk about where and how I got the book, how it relates to other things I've read, what sort of reactions it triggered in me (and why), and how one can get a copy if it sounds appealing. Needless to say, if the reader is devoted to standard book reviewing styles, this might be an irritation … however, it does make these reviews somewhat idiosyncratic to *me*, resulting in a collection that is something of a "my encounters with books" sort of deal, which will, hopefully, be appealing to many.

- Brendan Tripp

# CONTENTS

1 - Saturday, January 4, 2014

*Memory Lane ...*

**Everyday Book Marketing:
Promotion ideas to fit your regularly scheduled life**

by Midge Raymond

4 - Monday, January 6, 2014

*Three fingers back ...*

**Why the World Doesn't Seem to Make Sense:
An Inquiry into Science, Philosophy, and Perception**

by Steve Hagen

7 - Thursday, January 16, 2014

*Got a condo made of stone-a ...*

**Egyptomania: Our Three Thousand Year
Obsession with the Land of the Pharaohs**

by Bob Brier

10 - Friday, January 17, 2014

*Who do you trust?*

**Highly Recommended: Harnessing the Power of Word of Mouth
and Social Media to Build Your Brand and Your Business**

by Paul M. Rand

13 - Saturday, January 18, 2014

*And not a candlestick in sight ...*

**Quick and Nimble: Lessons from Leading CEOs
on How to Create a Culture of Innovation**

by Adam Bryant

16 - Sunday, January 19, 2014

*The CliffsNotes to social?*

**Maximize Your Social: A One-Stop Guide to Building a Social Media Strategy for Marketing and Business Success**

by Neal Schaffer

18 - Wednesday, February 19, 2014

*And here again ...*
### Essence of the Dhammapada:
### The Buddha's Call to Nirvana
by Eknath Easwaran

21 - Wednesday, March 5, 2014

*Why only half the story?*
### Losing Our Religion:
### The Liberal Media's Attack on Christianity
by S.E. Cupp

24 - Friday, March 7, 2014

*Absolutely smashing ...*
### Present at the Creation:
### the Story of CERN and the Large Hadron Collider
by Amir D. Aczel

27 - Saturday, April 5, 2014

*This may BE your grandfather's freaky ...*
### One Simple Idea:
### How Positive Thinking Reshaped Modern Life
by Mitch Horowitz

30 - Sunday, April 6, 2014

*Quite Revealing ...*
### The Demon Under the Microscope:
### From Battlefield Hospitals to Nazi Labs, One Doctor's
### Heroic Search for the World's First Miracle Drug
by Thomas Hager

33 - Thursday, May 1, 2014

*Letting your freak flag fly ...*
### The Freaks Shall Inherit the Earth: Entrepreneurship
### for Weirdos, Misfits, and World Dominators
by Chris Brogan

36 - Saturday, May 10, 2014

*The evolution of MarComm ...*

**Spin Sucks: Communication and
Reputation Management in the Digital Age**

by Gini Dietrich

39 - Monday, May 12, 2014

*Another green read ...*

**Biodiesel America: How to Achieve Energy Security,
Free America from Middle-east Oil Dependence
And Make Money Growing Fuel**

by Josh Tickell

42 - Saturday, May 17, 2014

*Say you're the CEO of a large corporation ...*

**How Excellent Companies Avoid Dumb Things:
Breaking the 8 Hidden Barriers
that Plague Even the Best Businesses**

by Neil Smith

45 - Sunday, May 18, 2014

*Escaping the old paradigm's cage ...*

**The Icarus Deception: How High Will You Fly?**

by Seth Godin

49 - Saturday, May 24, 2014

*Frankly, I prefer the Patti Smith version ...*

**Free Money "They" Don't Want You to Know About**

by Kevin Trudeau

52 - Sunday, May 25, 2014

*As platforms change ...*

**Likeable Social Media: How to Delight Your Customers,
Create an Irresistible Brand, and Be Generally Amazing
on Facebook (& Other Social Networks)**

by Dave Kerpen

55 - Saturday, June 21, 2014

*So modern ...*

**An Enemy of the People**

by Henrik Ibsen

58 - Sunday, June 22, 2014

*Yo-ho-ho ...*

**The Pirates' ~~Code~~ Guidelines: A Booke for Those Who Desire to Keep to the Code and Live a Pirate's Life**

by Joshamee Gibbs

60 - Saturday, July 12, 2014

*Once upon a time ...*

**Creativity, Inc.: Overcoming the Unseen Forces That Stand in the Way of True Inspiration**

by Ed Catmull

63 - Wednesday, July 23, 2014

*For a particular audience ...*

**Conscious Millionaire: Grow Your Business by Making a Difference**

by J.V. Crum, III

65 - Friday, July 25, 2014

*Sometimes things are worse than you imagined ...*

**Before the First Shots Are Fired: How America Can Win Or Lose Off The Battlefield**

by General Tony Zinni

68 - Sunday, July 27, 2014

*Psi statistical analysis ...*

**The Conscious Universe: The Scientific Truth of Psychic Phenomena**

by Dean Radin

71 - Monday, July 28, 2014

*An oldie, but still a goodie ...*

**Unleashing the Ideavirus: Stop Marketing AT People!
Turn Your Ideas into Epidemics by Helping
Your Customers Do the Marketing thing for You**

by Seth Godin

74 - Saturday, August 9, 2014

*Shaken, not stirred?*

**Startup Mixology: Tech Cocktail's Guide to
Building, Growing, and Celebrating Startup Success**

by Frank Gruber

77 - Sunday, August 10, 2014

*"It ain't what you want, it's what you need."*

**The Fortune Cookie Chronicles:
Adventures in the World of Chinese Food**

by Jennifer 8. Lee

80 - Monday, August 25, 2014

*Interesting, but very biased ...*

**Shortcut: How Analogies Reveal Connections,
Spark Innovation, and Sell Our Greatest Ideas**

by John Pollack

83 - Saturday, September 6, 2014

*"Free" ... tasting of reality*

**Free: The Future of a Radical Price**

by Chris Anderson

86 - Sunday, September 7, 2014

*How the big boys are doing social ...*

**The Social Employee:
How Great Companies Make Social Media Work**

by Cheryl & Mark Burgess

90 - Thursday, October 9, 2014

*On rosier planes ...*

**Riveted: The Science of Why Jokes Make Us Laugh, Movies Make Us Cry, and Religion Makes Us Feel One with the Universe**

by Jim Davies

93 - Saturday, October 11, 2014

*A difficult subject ...*

**Border Insecurity: Why Big Money, Fences, and Drones Aren't Making Us Safer**

by Sylvia Longmire

96 - Tuesday, October 21, 2014

*Connecting with the customer ...*

**UnSelling: The New Customer Experience**

by Scott Stratten

99 - Wednesday, October 22, 2014

*The problem with "used" ...*

**The Zen of Social Media Marketing: An Easier Way to Build Credibility, Generate Buzz, and Increase Revenue**

by Shama Hyder Kabani

102 - Monday, October 27, 2014

*And if they're Northern ...*

**The Ancestral Mind: Reclaim the Power**

by Dr. Gregg Jacobs

106 - Tuesday, October 28, 2014

*Spontaneous, creative ...*

**Impromptu Man: J.L. Moreno and the Origins of Psychodrama, Encounter Culture, and the Social Network**

by Jonathan D. Moreno

109 - Saturday, November 15, 2014

*Lives in "interesting times" ...*

**The Foremost Good Fortune**

by Susan Conley

111 - Sunday, November 16, 2014

*The ABCs of early Godin ...*

**Small Is the New Big: and 183 Other Riffs, Rants, and Remarkable Business Ideas**

by Seth Godin

114 - Saturday, December 6, 2014

*Bleh ...*

**The Nature of Reality: Akashic Guidance for Understanding Life and Its Purpose**

by Aingeal Rose O'Grady

117 - Sunday, December 7, 2014

*This actually helped ...*

**Spontaneous Happiness**

by Andrew Weil

121 - **QR Code Links**

133 - **Contents - Alphabetical By Author**

137 - **Contents - Alphabetical By Title**

Saturday, January 4, 2014[1]

# Memory Lane ...

As long-time readers of these reviews know, I've been involved in LibraryThing.com's "Early Reviewer" program for *years*. This is a benefit for membership on the LT site, where every month there are a hundred or so books made available by publishers, and one can put in requests for as many as one finds interesting (I typically average around 3-4 requests) and "The Almighty Algorithm" matches the book info the publishers provide with the meta data of one's LT collection, with the idea that this will match up the "best" person to review the book. I've only missed out on getting a book a few times over the past several years, and that happening usually when I only requested *one* book.

Needless to say, this is an LTER book, from September's batch (I'm actually backed up on several LTER books, so you'll be seeing a lot of them in here as I get caught up). Given that I used to run my own publishing company, it was no surprise that I ended up getting Midge Raymond's Everyday Book Marketing: Promotion ideas to fit your regularly scheduled life[2], but it does make one wonder how the Almighty Algorithm *knew* that, given that I really don't have that many "books about publishing" in my collection.

Of course, having *been* a publisher (and responsible for all of our "book marketing"), I came to this with a bit of a different context than many would. In the introductory material Raymond notes that she wrote this book specifically for the individual writer, one who has a book or two out, not the "aspiring" writer so much, and certainly not for the publishers out there (although much of the material here would be quite helpful for the small press looking to boost its authors' sales). The focus in on writers who have "other lives", jobs and families, and the responsibilities that come with those ... and tries to guide them on the path of becoming "marketing experts" in the hours they can dedicate to promoting their books.

Everyday Book Marketing[3] in in two parts, roughly half-and-half, with the first being a "this is what you should be doing" instructional piece, and the second being interviews with 18 ladies involved in the book business, both authors and publishing/promotion folks. I did find it interesting that there wasn't a guy in there ... unless the publishing business has changed greatly since I was involved (it's been about a decade at this point), that's probably an intentional thing making me think that this book is meant for *women* writers specifically ... although I may just being petty in that observation.

In the first half of the book, the material is presented in a fairly straightforward time line, broke into three sections, "Think Outside The Book", which encourages the author to consider her project in terms of the publishing details, the nature of the audience, how best to reach those readers, what resources you will need to promote the book, and what activities will work best with one's individual strengths and time available. The "meat" of the book comes in the next section, "First Things First: Book Marketing Basics", which is largely a step-by-step list of things to do prior to publication:

Align your publishing method with your goals.

- Take an author photo.
- Create an author bio.
- Create a website.
- Create visuals and giveaways.
- Start a blog.
- Develop a mailing list.
- Set up Google Alerts.
- Join and be active on social networks.
- Set up a book tour.
- A virtual book tour.
- Book clubs.
- Consider a book trailer.

Several of these topics are further divided into elements of the main piece – such as book tours and social media – but they all get pretty "granular" with, for instance, a list of pages to create on a web site, and sources for post cards, stickers, and buttons in "visuals and giveaways". The third section of the first half is "Book Launch and Beyond", which goes through activating things that were set up in previous sections, getting the press kit out, setting up an Amazon author page, going out on the book tour, and keeping things going from there.

The second half of the book features a dozen authors, a publicist, a photographer, a book blogger, and three "events" gals from various contexts. These vary in usefulness (I had a sense that a few were just in here because they were friends of Raymond's), but there was one really remarkable bit by author Kim Wright, responding to a question about the biggest challenge she'd encountered in marketing her books:

> The single biggest challenge facing all writers, whether they write fiction or nonfiction, whether they're conventionally published or self-published, is precisely the same: finding a readership.
>
> It used to be that the question facing writers was "Can I get published?" People were obsessed with finding an agent, then praying that the agent could sell the book. It was a narrow gate. Not a lot of people got through it, but those who did could expect that once they were on the other side they could get significant help from their editors, agents, and publishers.
>
> Now that's no longer the question. With the advent of self-publishing and the fact that most

> *readers are shopping online for books and the whole e-book explosion ... it's a different world. I always say the good news is that anybody can get published. And the bad news is that anybody can get published. Because there are so many books in the marketplace – more than six times as many now published per year as there were two years ago. And there certainly aren't six times as many readers.*
>
> *So the question is not "Can I get published?" but "Once I get published, what do I need to do to help my book succeed?" The challenge is standing out in an oversaturated market, and I think that's a matter of knowing who your target readers are, where and how they shop for books, and tailoring your strategies to make it easy for them to discover your books.*

That certainly is key advice for anybody in the publishing universe! Frankly, the whole of <u>Everyday Book Marketing</u>[4] would be a useful lesson for anybody going into "the book biz", as there are so many hints to avoid pitfalls and take advantage of unsuspected opportunities (like making yourself available to area organizations related to the subject of your book), all through it – both in the "instructions" and in the "interviews" halves. This just came out a couple of months back, so is likely to be available out in the more comprehensive surviving brick-and-mortar book vendors, and it can be found at a bit of a discount via the on-line big boys. While I had some issues with this, I found the material reasonably solid and actionable, so would not hesitate to recommend it to an author looking to get involved with active book promotion. I know that there are things in here that I *wish* I could have gotten my authors to do on a regular basis back when I had my press, and there are things (like virtual tours) which are new since those days which would have certainly helped.

Notes:

1. http://btripp-books.livejournal.com/152111.html

2-4. http://amzn.to/1Fi9JWD

Monday, January 6, 2014[1]

# Three fingers back ...

I had great hopes for this book when I "won" it in the LibraryThing.com "Early Reviewer" program ... it sounded like the sort of cognition/cosmology sort of thing that I've not indulged in for a while, but read a great deal of previously. Steve Hagen's Why the World Doesn't Seem to Make Sense: An Inquiry into Science, Philosophy, and Perception[2] *seemed* to have all the requisite elements in place (down to an M.C. Escher illustration on the cover), but I never quite got "traction" with it.

Now, I am perfectly willing to posit that I "just didn't *get* it" ... there are several areas of study where I, despite many sorties against their walls over the years, still find largely impenetrable (music theory being one irritatingly notable example), and, of course, what may be one person's perfectly cogent explanation/discussion of some reasonably esoteric subject will sometimes end up being random *blah-blah-blah* to another's ears/eyes.

The author here is a long-time student of Zen, who has been an ordained Zen priest since 1979, the carrier of the Dharma transmission from his teacher, Katagiri Roshi, for the past quarter century, the founder of Dharma Field[3] in Minneapolis, MN, and has written several books on Buddhism. I don't recall there being any biographical information on his having a background in either science or philosophy ... which probably points to one thing that I found difficult with his book ... he keeps wrestling with fairly obscure Zen technical points, and then extrapolating them into general philosophical positions, and then using that to *combat* assorted stances of science ... which don't (from where I'm sitting) really need being attacked.

Frankly, much of this book reminds me of a *Christian fundamentalist* having a reasonably clueless go at some established scientific theory, just because it "doesn't support" his theology/mythology. In this case, most of the time it seems that Hagen is railing against things because they don't conform to, or filter through, some particular Zen/philosophical template. Again, I am willing to cede the concept that I might be simply not able to fully comprehend the finer points of his arguments, but it does remind me of strident types selling other religions who just can't get off their favored doctrine points ... which appear, for this author, to be "Paradox and Confusion" as "guardians of Truth", framed in a context that *"Something is tragically wrong with the human world. ... we're rushing headlong toward some great calamity ..."* and the question: *"Why this apparent madness to human life"?*.

It might be useful to take a walk through the chapter headings to see the general arc of his argument. The book is in three parts, "Nobody Knows What's Going On", featuring Belief, Knowledge, Contradiction, and Certitude, "At Ease With Inconceivability", with Chaos, Consciousness, and Immediacy, and "What Matters" presenting Inertia, Becoming, and Totality, all of which are further subdivided into topical sections. While this *looks* to be a reasonably coherent movement, I found it very hard to follow, as he would weave in and out of *scientific* elements with which I was very familiar, some general Zen material that I knew well enough, and even philosophical whirlpools where I could at least track trajectories, but it would always come back to stuff like this:

> There are two aspects of our existence. One is called "this is it" - the this, the "something", or r aspect. It's here that we exist as separate entities, in a particular place, at a certain time.
>
> But we must not forget that there is another aspect called "what is it?" - the what, the "nothing", or i aspect. The two aspects are interrelated and interpenetrated; they are like a seiche, the back-and-forth movement of liquid in a basin. A seiche constantly spills out of itself and its "other", only to slosh back. The r and i aspects are also like a graded stream, where as soon as something in the system changes, everything else in the system – which involves stars and galaxies, as Bell's Theorem demonstrates – begins to move to counter the effect of the change.
>
> So, when we ask, "what is it?" we can only point to "here it is". "This", is all we can say. It – whatever "it" happens to be – constantly exchanges its identity with every other thing. This is how we live. We live in a Reality that is like music, like a graded stream, or like the sloshing of liquid within a basin. We "exist" not in **being** but in becoming – and in fading away.
>
> Within one aspect of our lives – the common, bounded, this aspect – we each have separate identities. But we must also accept that "other" aspect that reveals no boundary. Given this other aspect, each object and each person is intimately connected (indeed, is interidentical) with everything that ever was and ever will be, no matter how distant it appears in space or time.
>
> Once we realize this other aspect of Reality, we can see that there's something more to human life than mere phenomenal existence. There's something vast, wonderful, and unbounded. There's a deep relationship, a grand symbiosis, and interidentity of the Whole and the part.

Yes, this is a grand sweep of verbiage that basically is working its way back to *Tat Tvam Asi*, through various strange side streets featuring Bell's Theorem, Schrodinger's Cat, the Mandelbrot Set, and Nagarjuna's "tetralemma" … unfortunately losing me on the way. While I suspect I might have an idea what he means when he gets to *"seeing"*, but his "proof", if you will, by which he arrives there largely escapes me.

> Our task is to just see. Our direct experience – i.e., perception itself – is the Undefined that says with unimpeachable authority that all things appear not in being, but in becoming and in fading away.

So, what to say about Why the World Doesn't Seem to Make Sense[4]? … it's a revision of a book that Hagen put out 17 years previously, which he frames as having been detailing elements *"about consciousness that science continues to overlook"*, one gets the sense that he "reloaded" with more bits of physics and cosmology, and decided to charge the windmills again with this one. While I was fascinated with *parts* of this, I found it uneven, and frequently (with its *r*'s and *i*'s) beating something dead that I was only able to assume was a horse. You, however, might not have the same perceptions of this that I had, so you might like it better. This has been out for a year, so might be scarce in the stores, and I'm rather surprised that the online new/used guys don't have it at a significant discount at this point. If you're into *philosophical* rabbit-holing (with a Zen axe to grind), you will no doubt find this engaging, but, to me, it never quite got around to making sense.

Notes:

1. http://btripp-books.livejournal.com/152374.html
2. http://amzn.to/1Fi9laO
3. http://dharmafield.org/
4. http://amzn.to/1Fi9laO

Thursday, January 16, 2014[1]

# Got a condo made of stone-a ...

I suppose that I should stop being *surprised* when books that I get via the LibraryThing.com "Early Reviewers" program aren't exactly what I had anticipated them to be when I clicked that "Request it!" link. After all, these are (usually) new books coming out, for which the publishers are looking to get some "early" buzz working. This means that I pretty much only have the paragraph or so of promo copy in the listing to make a decision on whether or not I'd be interested in reading/reviewing a particular title.

It's not that Bob Brier's Egyptomania: Our Three Thousand Year Obsession with the Land of the Pharaohs[2] had a *misleading* blurb ... but this *"inventive and mesmerizing tour of how an ancient civilization endures in ours today"* sounded like it was going to be more, well, *serious* than it ended up. Perhaps my confusion on that point was influenced by the famed Zahi Hawass providing an Introduction here. Hawass is well known for his toeing the "official Egyptological line" in all things (especially in contrast to any new age or alternative timeline views), but maybe his removal as Minister of Antiquities in the wake of the overthrow of Mubarak has left him at loose ends and he's become more amenable to expanding his repertoire.

What I was expecting was more along the line of *cultural* survivals of Egyptian elements, from architectural residuals (which there are several noted here), to "secret societies'" appropriation of the images and vocabulary, to perhaps even reflections on just how deeply the Christian mythos is intertwined with the figures of Isis, Horus, Osiris, and Set ... but this doesn't delve into those fascinating topics, but concentrates largely on Egyptian *stuff* ... from the acquisition of various monuments to the predictable explosion of Egyptian-themed *kitch* every time something comes up to thrust the (ancient) Egyptians into the Western cultural groupthink.

The author, Bob Brier, is noted to have *"been amassing one of the largest collections of Egyptian memorabilia"* for the past forty years, but his resume seems pretty thin on actual Egyptology, with degrees in Philosophy and *Parapsychology* (not that I'm the type to diss Psi research, but still), and he's been teaching at Long Island University since the early 70s. He has spent a long time studying mummification, and has even performed this arcane art on a cadaver in 1994 ... but he seems to be more in the "enthusiastic amateur" mold (with a good travel budget) who has visited a lot of sites, than somebody who's done seasons with a spade from the archaeological side.

This goes a long way to explain why the book is full of *tchotchkes*, antique advertising, and assorted ephemera, and not with more substantial cultural concerns. Now, to be fair, the book *does* attempt to make a historical survey of the influence of Egypt in Western culture. From the Greeks, with Herodotus tracing *"almost all aspects of Greek civilization back to the Egyptians"*, and Alexander conquering Egypt and making it the jewel of his empire, and on through the fascination and integration that Rome brought to the subject (from the empire-wide popularizing of the Isis cult to the notorious extinguishing of the Ptolemaic dynasty by Julius Caesar and Mark Antony).

Nearly half the book is taken up with stories of how the assorted obelisks made their way from Egypt to Rome, Paris, London, and New York. Rome's came early, having been imported by Caligula in 37 c.e., and was a fixture of his (and Nero's) circus – which used to be right about where Vatican City sits. Aside for noting that in 391 c.e., (Christian) Emperor Theodosius I decreed that all Egyptian temples be closed (with the last hieroglyphic inscription being made in 394), the next part of this history comes in 1585 c.e., when the original version of St. Peter's Basilica was being re-built, and moved from its original site. After having that obelisk sitting in its front yard (as it were) for over 1,000 years, the Church decided it had to be moved to the new site, and this was accomplished by one Domenico Fontana in 1586, *"considered one of the great engineering feats of the Renaissance"*.

One of the most *fascinating* parts of Egyptomania[3] is the material regarding Napoleon Bonaparte, very little of it particularly complimentary. In 1798 he opted out of an assignment to directly attack England, and instead convinced the revolutionary Directory to send him to Egypt (like his hero Alexander) to attack British interests there. To his credit, Napoleon brought a large contingent of academics and engineers, from whose researches we have the baseline scholarly knowledge of Egypt. The Egyptian campaign did not go particularly well, and Napoleon abandoned his army, returned to France, and minted medallions celebrating his triumph.

Situations in Egypt were somewhat chaotic, as the British, after chasing off the remnants of Napoleon's forces, pretty much just packed up and headed home. Egyptian rulers offered obelisks to a whole succession of British monarchs, to no result, and they eventually offered them to France ... since many French savants had been in Egypt, they jumped at the chance, and in 1836 the first of these arrived in Paris.

The Brits, of course, suddenly realized that they'd been missing out on this obelisk stuff, and a *commercial* venture was assembled to bring one to London. A submarine-like cylinder of a ship was built in 1877 to carry the obelisk, and it was to be towed through the Mediterranean and up Europe's Atlantic coast and on to England. Unfortunately, the weather was not cooperating and in an October storm, a number of crew died trying to secure the ship, which was lost. Lost, but not sunk, and it was claimed as salvage a short time later, and "ransomed" through the courts. The obelisk finally was raised in London in September 1878 ... sparking a massive wave of Victorian "Egyptomania" with nearly endless Egyptian-themed stuff and ads clearly made by the clueless for consumers with no more idea of what the "real" Egypt looked like!

American interests were already angling for an obelisk, and one was arranged for in 1878, but it took nearly three years to get it set up in Central Park, with the installation coming in February of 1881. At least the New York contingent had learned from the French and British, as the engineering had been well thought-through to not only get the obelisk across the ocean, but into the center of the city. Interestingly, the Masons had a lot to do with this one, and there were supposedly Masonic items found in the base in Egypt, and they were a significant part of the events connected to raising it – although the Grand Master very clearly noted that there were no Freemasons around that far back.

Of course, the biggest blasts of "Egyptomania" followed the discovery of Tutankhamen's tomb in 1922, leading to products, music, films, fashion, etc. This was echoed again when, in the 1970's the *Treasures of Tutankhamen* exhibit went on tour, with more products, and music like Steve Martin's "King Tut". The movies started in 1923 and haven't let up, with mummy-themed movie following mummy-themed movie for the past 90 years … these are also looked at here in detail.

Anyway, while Egyptomania[4] wasn't the book that I'd sort of hoped it might be, there was certainly plenty of very interesting stuff the I'd never encountered previously to keep me engaged. I could have done with less of the "cultural kitsch", but I guess that's what's in the author's collection, so there are a hundred or so illustrations … handy, I suppose, if you had an itch to know what the cover art for the "Cleopatra Had A Jazz Band" sheet music looked like in the 20's. This has just been out a couple of months so it's likely findable out in the more pop-culture oriented brick-and-mortars, but the online big boys have it at a significant discount. The read provided lots of "I did *not* know that!" moments, but even more "Did I *need* to know that?" stuff in here – yet fans of Antique Road Show may love it.

Notes:

1. http://btripp-books.livejournal.com/152754.html
2-4. http://amzn.to/1dbms4C

Friday, January 17, 2014[1]

# Who do you trust?

I have to predicate this review with a bit more "disclosure" than I usually do ... I've known author Paul M. Rand for a while, and even interviewed with him a couple of years ago for a position at his agency, the Zócalo Group (sadly, I didn't get hired). This past summer, he gave a presentation at Social Media Week Chicago where he previewed the book ... and while I wasn't able to make that session, the buzz it created was notable, as I kept running into folks at the various parties who were talking about it. Of course, I hopped onto Gmail and sent off a request to the good folks at McGraw-Hill for a review copy of Highly Recommended: Harnessing the Power of Word of Mouth and Social Media to Build Your Brand and Your Business[2] which they kindly sent along when the book came out.

Rand's Zócalo was one of the early agencies focusing on "word of mouth" campaigns, and this is, naturally, the focus of the book. The currency of word-of-mouth marketing is the "recommendation", and the dynamic of this is boiled down to one question on the inner flap of the dust jacket: *"What do you trust more – an advertisement or a friend?"* ... followed up by a factoid from Nielsen that the top reason reported by 92% of consumers of what influenced them to buy a product or service was a word of mouth recommendation.

In the Preface, Rand defines what he's intending for the book:

> *Social media has supercharged the power and impact of recommendations. Today's businesses can't just <u>use</u> social media; they have to become social businesses, inside and out and from top to bottom. Ultimately, that is the goal of this book: to harness the power of being a social business to become the most highly recommended organization in your industry, category, and/or niche. The ability to easily research online consumer reviews or see which brands your social media friends like is fundamentally shifting how people buy – and sell – nearly everything.*

This, while providing *"an easy way for marketers to understand and act upon making their brand eminently "talkable", shareable, and recommended".* He's divided the book into three roughly even parts, the first on the theory, the second on the how-to, and a third on transforming your business.

It could be argued that Highly Recommended[3] is an outgrowth of a Convocation Address that Rand gave at Northwestern back in 2012, Living A Recommendable Life[4], which is presented in its entirety in the Introduction, the key points of which are:

1. Develop a clear and purposeful story of how you want people to talk about and recommend both you and your brands.
2. Live your brand.
3. Be human, be transparent, and live up to mistakes quickly.
4. Stay engaging and interesting.
5. Regularly evaluate and evolve – but stay true to your core.

However, that piece is about as "philosophical" as it gets, and the rest is a combination of personal stories and *fire hose* info. Rand starts with an example ... he's on a business trip, and he's meeting with clients, and at dinner the subject of a supermarket chain called Stew Leonard's comes up and he indicates that he'd never heard of them (they just have 4 locations), and is *regaled* by these clients for the next 30 minutes with story after story after story of how awesome this company is, and both these businesswomen offered to pick him up early before their morning meetings so they could *show* him this amazing place. As he notes, *"it was a microcourse ... about how the recommendation culture worked, the power of recommendations, the passion of advocacy, and the motivation behind helping others through suggestion"*.

He has stories about Angie's List, Yelp, and others to give concrete, relatable examples of how the theory works, and then breaks down the theory into sub-sections such as "Are You Engaging Your Audience – or Interrupting Them?", while supporting things with sources such as Robert Cialdini's *Influence* and Bill Lee's assorted pieces positing that "Marketing is Dead". He warns that "creeping your customers out" with too much "Big Brother" big data is the next danger zone (I know I hate seeing stuff I surfed for online showing up as ads elsewhere on the web!) in the "consumer decision journey", while defining such things as a "loyalty loop". He dissects the math behind the "Net Promoter Score" and how that relates to Zócalo's own "Recommendation Index", discusses the differences between Explicit and Implied endorsements, and walks the reader through some case studies and on into the "Influencer Ecosystem". My head's still spinning from just flipping through that again.

Next he moves into the nuts-and-bolts part, discussing free and paid tools for monitoring and managing word-of-mouth, and then introduces Zócalo's "Digital Footprint Analysis", which is based on "Four W's":

- **Who** – Who's talking?
- **What** – What are they saying?
- **Where** – Where are these conversations taking place?
- **Why** – Why does this matter?

This is followed with how to plan, how best to include SEO, how to develop a "Shareable Story Map" with examples from projects he's done, and how to integrate Paid, Owned, Earned, and Shared media and strategies within the "path to recommendation", and finally looks at how to *defend* your brand against hostile/negative word-of-mouth. Amazingly, he cites studies that as many as 67% of consumers *won't buy* a product if it has as few as three negative reviews, which makes the "Determined Detractors" (in three flavors: "Hear Me's", "Reputation Terrorists", and "Competitive Destroyers") a real hazard. Rand goes into detail on how to deal with these various types of risks, and how to be proactive with one's listening and messaging.

The final part of the book is interesting as it's sort of a manual for re-making one's business to be more "recommendable", looking at customer service, HR and staffing issues, product innovation and R&D, and how to bring all those elements into an integrated whole. Obviously, this is more of a "specialized" concern (I could make use of a lot of the previous sections' stuff, but don't have a company I'm currently running to implement these bits), but some of the stories there are amazing, like the user on the "CloroxConnects" service who shared a dozen solid product ideas in less than a year, and how customer engagement has resulted in numerous new product pushes at several major corporations.

Obviously, Highly Recommended[5] isn't a "general reader" book, but if you have an interest in marketing, social media, and the evolving communication channels, this will be a riveting read. The combination of personal stories and textbook-like detailing of the elements being discussed provides an engaging and *highly* informative intro to word-of-mouth marketing. This has been out a few months, but I'm guessing it's selling well enough that all the business-oriented brick-and-mortar stores will have this stocked, but the usual suspects online are currently offering it for about 1/3rd off cover price, if you want to go that route. I really got a lot out of reading this one, and it's probably the best "primer" for the WOM niche since Andy Sernovitz's Word of Mouth Marketing[6] which sort of defined the space a couple of years back!

Notes:

1. http://btripp-books.livejournal.com/152982.html
2-3. http://amzn.to/1HIQHiZ
4. http://zocalogroup.com/wp-content/uploads/2012/06/Living-a-Recommendable-Life-by-Paul-M.pdf
5. 3http://amzn.to/1HIQHiZ
6. http://btripp-books.livejournal.com/134737.html

Saturday, January 18, 2014[1]

# And not a candlestick in sight ...

I suppose that one of the nice things about the Library-Thing.com "Early Reviewer" program is that it's like a grab-bag gift exchange, but instead of the shape of the item, and how it's wrapped, the way you end up guessing what you're going to like is the paragraph or so of promo copy that the publishers provide about the book. Yes, you're *way* ahead of the game vs. a "pig in a poke" pick-a-gift in that you *sort of* know what you're getting ... but I'm finding that I'm only rarely reading the book *I thought* I was requesting. Today's title is another example of this.

Now, I guess if I had heard of the author, or of his *New York Times* column, or previous book, I might have had a better sense of what was coming. But when the description said that Adam Bryant had interviewed "more than two hundred" (a figure that keeps coming up, even though less than 150 seem to have actually made it into the book) CEOs for this, I figured that Quick and Nimble: Lessons from Leading CEOs on How to Create a Culture of Innovation[2] was going to be a series of interviews (or highlights thereof) extracting from these leaders their *"wisdom and guidance to move an organization faster, to be quick and nimble, and to rekindle the whatever-it-takes collective spark of a start-up, all with the goal of innovating and thriving in a relentlessly challenging global economy"*. But it's not.

Frankly, what Bryant has done here is much easier to digest than what would have been the case were it to have been just interview after interview, but it took me a bit longer than half the book to come up with *a model* of what was going on in it. The material here is fascinating, and I was getting the feeling after each chapter that I'd just attended a really interesting seminar by top-notch experts on a particular subject ... and it struck me that this book was somewhat like a series of sixteen heavily-moderated (since everything is woven through Bryant's narration) panel presentations, each with a different mix of CEOs (although a few of them keep showing up across the book), and each chapter pretty much free-standing like that.

Now, had I had *that* perception going in, I might have gotten more from the earlier parts, when I was still trying to "figure it out" ... I kept finding myself enjoying the book when actually reading it, but having a hard time picking it up in favor of other things I was reading (although I must admit, I did finish this first of the three books I started reading in the first week of January). Given this, it might be useful to walk through Quick and Nimble's[3] chapters (with a brief note on my take on the "theme" of each) to see what these "expert panel seminars" are discussing:

1. *Why Culture Matters ("culture eats strategy for breakfast")*
2. *A Simple Plan (mission statements, measurable goals, etc.)*
3. *Rules of the Road (values that steer your company)*

4. *A Little Respect (bad bosses and behaviors)*
5. *It's About the Team (working together, relying on each other)*
6. *Adult Conversations ("tough love" for the greater good)*
7. *The Hazards of E-mail (easy to misinterpret, easy to abuse)*
8. *Play It Again and Again (constantly communicating)*
9. *Building Better Managers (not everybody comes equipped)*
10. *Surfacing Problems (researching how things really work in-house)*
11. *School Never Ends (not growing = dying)*
12. *The Art of Smarter Meetings (optimizing those sometimes-necessary evils)*
13. *Knocking Down Silos (how to avoid tribalism)*
14. *Sparking Innovation (keeping things fresh, and hungry)*
15. *Can We Have Some Fun? (some silliness solidifies solidarity)*
16. *Alone at the Top (trust, urgency, and change)*

Again, there are a lot of voices here, perhaps a dozen or more on some of these, so there's more of a "lively give-and-take" than a definitive statement in any ... although, obviously, the author is constructing a pathway to a particular point with each. Because of this structure, I found it difficult to pinpoint specific statements to hold out as illustrative of their subjects. I did, however, end up bookmarking a couple of things that somewhat stood out to me.

One of these is sort of second-hand, coming from AOL's Steve Case, but in this quoting a fellow founder of the online service, Jim Kimsey. Case says that his view in the early part of his career was that *"looking like you're working hard mattered"*, but he relates Kimsey's insistence that *"the art is trying to set the priorities and assemble a team so you wake up in the morning and actually have nothing to do"*. He continues with:

> *The objective should not be looking busy, but actually creating a process that allows great things to happen in a way that you can be less involved. So it was sort of a process of letting go, which is hard for entrepreneurs. But at some point you've got to let go and you've got to step back. Ultimately that is about trusting the people you've got but also trusting yourself, that you've set the right context in terms of the vision, the priorities, the team.*

I don't think anybody would be surprised that this is the opening part of the "Alone at the Top" chapter, but it's a good sampling of the sort of material that fills [Quick and Nimble](#)[4]. Some of it runs close to "common wisdom", what' you'd expect, but a good deal goes counter to what one would guess to work best.

One other quote that stood out here was in this category, coming from Marcus Ryu of Guidewire, from the "Play It Again and Again" chapter:

> *Even though we talk about how important rationality is in the company, I've come to accept that rationality plays a very limited role in persuasion, and that it's mostly about emotion. It's mostly about empathy and about authenticity and about commitment. ... {S}ort of a corollary to that, is about communicating with large groups of people. I've come to realize that no matter how smart the people are that you're communicating to, the more of them there are, the dumber the collective gets. And so you could have a room full of Einsteins, but if there are two hundred or three hundred of them, then you still have to talk to them like they're just average people. As the audience gets bigger and bigger, the bullet-point list has to be shorter and shorter, and the messages have to be simpler and simpler.*

Which is, I guess, a more round-about way to get to the classic "KISS" advice for Keeping It Simple.

Anyway, as noted, reading Quick and Nimble[5] is very much like sitting through a series of top-talent panel-based seminars, with input from a remarkable selection of CEOs across a very wide assortment of industries, and I almost feel like one should get a certificate for finishing it (not that the book is a *difficult* read by any measure). This has been out for less than two weeks at this point, so you should be find it in the "new releases" sections of the remaining business-oriented brick-and-mortar book vendors, but the on-line behemoths *are* currently knocking off a quarter of the cover price on the hardback. Anybody with an interest in business, marketing, and innovation should consider picking this up ... it's quite the experience!

Notes:

1. http://btripp-books.livejournal.com/153225.html
2-5. http://amzn.to/1Fi7Zga

Sunday, January 19, 2014[1]

# The CliffsNotes to social?

Last fall, I'd noticed Neal Schaffer posting a lot out on social media channels about his new book, Maximize Your Social: A One-Stop Guide to Building a Social Media Strategy for Marketing and Business Success[2], so I hopped on email and requested the good folks at Wiley to send me a review copy. While I got around to *reading* it fairly quickly, for some reason it's been languishing in the lower levels of my to-be-reviewed pile, until coming up now, a couple of months down the road, when I'm getting caught up on that backlog.

I *really* prefer to review books within a week or so of finishing them, so this isn't as "fresh" as it ought to be ... fortunately, I do have something like a dozen bookmarks in it, so I've got points to reference.

The over-view of Maximize Your Social[3] is pretty straight forward ... it is, as the subtitle suggests, a "one-stop guide", which pretty much means it's trying to be "soup-to-nuts" in the Social Media sphere. But this is a relatively thin volume (especially if compared to Lon Safko's massive *Social Media Bible*), around 200 pages to cover 18 subjects, so it presents more breadth than depth, generally speaking.

Of course, this is not inherently a bad thing ... if one were an "old school" marketer, and managed to "miss" that whole Internet thing and those Social Media sites the kids were messing around with, this would be an easy to digest walk-through of pretty much every element of social media marketing. And it's not just for the clueless, as it has condensed into it a vast lot of tips, tricks, and hidden goodies that even seasoned social users might have missed (I don't believe, for instance, that I'd run into Facebook Insights before reading about it in here). One thing that I've already "borrowed" is his "four buckets" model for blog content – a company decides on four areas or themes that it would like to promote via Social, and comes up with one blog post each per month, thereby (fairly painlessly) keeping up a once-a-week posting frequency, while maintaining some variation in topics.

The focus is very much on setting up marketing strategies, and there are numerous "how-to" sections that give at least the main points on things like doing a "social media audit" that is certainly from the consulting side of Schaffer's business ... and probably not the first thing to come to mind for most people looking at expanding into the niche. He's obviously taken his own "cheat sheets" for things like Facebook engagement, with a list of five easy-to-execute ideas to build response on that platform, and worked them into the individual parts of the book.

The first quarter of the book does basic "backgrounding" on Social Media and how to use it in a marketing program. This then moves to specifics in the next quarter of the book with chapters that look at ways for "Maximizing" (his current branding concept) presences on Facebook, Twitter, LinkedIn, Google+, as well as blogs and "visual" channels such as Pinterest, Instagram, YouTube, etc. Now, there is a vast lot of information in these chapters, but it is necessarily briefly dealt with, as all six of those chapters only span 66 pages.

The last half of the book is really rather heavy into nuts-and-bolts of *running* social campaigns, which he casts in a PDCA "Deming cycle" of activities. These chapters break down as follows: "Determining Staffing Roles and Responsibilities", "Onboarding Your Social Media Strategy", "Managing the Risks", "Creating Your PDCA Workflow", "Integrating Your Social Media Strategy", and "The ROI of Your Social Media Strategy". In these he digs down pretty far into detail for how to set up teams, and even gets into Altimeter's research on typical distribution of resources (decentralized, centralized, hub and spoke, multiple hub and spoke, and "dandelion") and expounds further on those he sees as the main three models.

He also includes materials from other experts ... from a 7-page paper on Social Media Guidelines, a 5-page look at Google+ and SEO, on down to half-page pieces on "social media experimentation", etc. Some of these are expert-level advice and context, and quite valuable ... but they take up nearly half the page count of the second half of the book.

At one point in Maximize Your Social[4], Schaffer notes that he has a sales background ... and I think this explains a lot about the tone of the book. There's an affection for structures like the "PDCA Workflow" and less so for the creatives who would usually be handling social programs, and a "let's cut to the chase" sort of a feel here which reminds me of some network marketing "big dogs" I've known. On a lot of levels, this is an opposite approach to Social than say, Dave Kerpen's "Likeable" model, or Paul M. Rand's focus on becoming "recommendable" ... it's about how to get one's business from point A to point B, without necessarily caring about the process.

As I mentioned, there is LOT of useful material here, even for those who have been in Social for a long time ... but it's so condensed that it almost feels like reading the CliffsNotes on the field. The target audience for the book is clearly business managers/owners who want to make use of these new marketing tools, but have no idea how to start. If you're in that category, this would be a great way for you to jump into it. If you've come to Social from another angle, however, this has the potential to irritate. I appreciated the information flow in this, but was ultimately so-so on the book. It's only been out a few months, so the business book vendors no doubt still have it on the shelves, and, as usual, the on-line big boys are offering it at a discount. Again, this is not a *bad* book, and it would no doubt be a great intro for folks in the MBA ranks, but it occupies a particularly "sales-y" niche compared to most others dealing with social out there.

Notes:

1. http://btripp-books.livejournal.com/153588.html
2-4. http://amzn.to/1JnILQz

Wednesday, February 19, 2014[1]

# And here again ...

I very rarely re-read books intentionally, but the *Dhammapada* seems to be one of those books that ends up, in one form or another, finding its way into my reading pile every 2-3 years. Of course, I'm not *really* "re-reading" it, as I'm not going back to the same edition, and there is a great deal of difference given the background of the translator/interpreter, as well as when the book was produced. If you're interested, I have reviews of F. Max Müller's[2] translation (which was a Dover reprint of a book that was over a century old, notably featuring the unfortunate replacement of now-familiar terms *Dharma* and *Sangha* with the harsher "law" and "church"), and Juan Mascaro's[3] translation and excellent interpretive essay (itself probably influenced by its 1973 vintage).

Actually, Mascaro's book is a good bridge to the subject of this review, Eknath Easwaran's Essence of the Dhammapada: The Buddha's Call to Nirvana[4], as the present volume is more of a long "interpretive essay" than a translation. If the author's name rings a bell, it's because I reviewed his Essence of the Bhagavad Gita[5] a couple of years back. Like that book, this one came into my hands via the "Early Reviewers" program at LibraryThing.com ... so was not something that I particularly went in search of, but was quite happy to have obtained.

Eknath Easwaran has quite an interesting bio, having earned degrees in India in English and Law, and served as a Professor of English at his alma mater, the University of Nagpur, one of the top educational institutions there. At age 49 he was awarded a Fulbright scholarship, and moved to the USA, settling in at UC-Berkeley, where he started Meditation classes in 1960. Over the next several years he started the Blue Mountain Center, and the publishing operation, Nilgiri Press, which is responsible for this volume. He has published *dozens* of books over the decades, and, prior to his passing in 1999, he organized an on-going effort to get all of his unfinished volumes out to the public, of which these "Essence of" titles are examples.

It is arguable, that a figure such as Eknath Easwaran is *ideal* for bringing the Indian classics to a modern audience. Not only did he emerge from the cultural context from which they arose, but he spent most of his years directly working with the English language, *and* teaching meditation and associated practices.

I suppose that some might be unhappy that Essence of the Dhammapada[6] is not so much a direct *translation* of the teachings of the Buddha, but the insight, language, and perspective (very clear about the modern world) he brings to the material is exceptional.

> *Over and over again, the Buddha tells us we can all make the journey to nirvana – not by colossal*

> steps, not instantaneously, but little by little, every day, both during meditation and during our daily routine – at work, in the store, in the kitchen, at school, in the home. It's done slowly, gently, by taming the whims and caprices of the mind.

The concept of "taming the caprices of the mind" is a central theme here. The author speaks a lot about the challenges *he* experienced in learning to meditate, and, having taught these methods for decades, he knows where people get stuck, and how the mind tries to have its own way (another nice quote on the subject: *"Vigilance where the mind is concerned is one of the Buddha's favorite subjects."*).

Now, I'm not suggesting that this *ignores* the basic text ... bits and pieces of it are woven through the narrative ... but the author uses these more as thematic jumping-off points for discussing the underlying meaning than as a item-for-item walk-through. For example, he references this verse:

> Be like a well-trained horse, swift and spirited, and go beyond sorrow through faith, meditation, and energetic practice of the dharma. [144]

... when he is discussing key challenges in subduing the mind:

> Even if we accept that the mind can be trained, it's not going to be easy ... rather than riding on a swift steed to nirvana, to use the Buddha's image, we find we have a monkey mind as a companion on our journey ... a famous Sanskrit verse says this is a monkey that is drunk, stung by a scorpion, and possessed by a ghost – all at the same time.

The Essence of the Dhammapada[7] operates on several different levels. On one hand, it *is* an exposition of the key elements of the Buddha's teachings, but geared to a modern Western audience. It is also something of a spiritual autobiography, as the author dips into his history and experiences, to help guide, warn, and encourage the reader. And, there is a good deal of "philosophy" as well, using set-ups like: *When asked if the world is real, the Buddha says no. When asked if the world is unreal, the Buddha says no. Then what is the world? The Buddha says: "It is in between."* to move into a section discussing the concepts of the 2nd Century Mahayana teacher Nagarjuna.

I very much enjoyed reading The Essence of the Dhammapada[8], although it took me a very long time to get through it (this is the sort of book that one is likely need time to "process" as one works though it, instead of plowing through at top reading speed!). As one would expect from this being in the "Early Reviewers" program, it is quite new, having just come out a few months back, so it will likely be obtainable via the brick & mortar book mongers who carry religion/philosophy titles out there ... lacking one of those ever-more-rare sources, the on-line big boys have it. An additional thing to recommend this is its *very* reasonable cover price, which makes it quite painless to pick up. I liked this a lot, and am thankful that Eknath Easwaran arranged for its posthumous publication.

Notes:

1. http://btripp-books.livejournal.com/153612.html
2. http://btripp-books.livejournal.com/50529.html
3. http://btripp-books.livejournal.com/122307.html
4. http://amzn.to/1Hn3zs0
5. http://btripp-books.livejournal.com/127140.html
6-8. http://amzn.to/1Hn3zs0

Wednesday, March 5, 2014[1]

# Why only half the story?

I'm afraid that this review is likely to end up being more about *me* than it is about the source material. As regular readers will recognize, I'm both a conservative-leaning Libertarian politically, and a "deep agnostic" on the religion front ... being one of those "wishy-washy" near-atheists that irritate the likes of Penn Jillette. Frankly, I have studied so much religion that one could say I'm Vajrayana one day, a Pantheist the next, a paleo-Pagan Shaman the day after, a Gurdjieff/Ouspensky "Fourth Way" follower another, a Thelemite on occasion, a Sufi-esque mystic at times, and a hard-core scientific materialist every now and again (and I'm probably missing stuff here). This is where the agnostic/atheistic split comes in - it's not that I categorically deny the *possibility* of there being a deity along the lines of what the big three monotheisms envision, it's just that I consider that particular view only *slightly* more plausible than Bertram Russell's cosmic teapot[2]. Or, as Christopher Hitchens put it: *"Since it is obviously inconceivable that all religions can be right, the most reasonable conclusion is that they are all wrong."*!

I venture into this bit of autobiographical digression to frame what brought me to the current book. I had not been familiar with S.E. Cupp (not making a habit of watching CNN or MSNBC where her shows are), but ran across a mention of her as being both a conservative *and* an atheist ... and I'm always eager to find "fellow travelers" down the somewhat lonely path (although I find that many Libertarians are sufficiently uninterested in dictating to others what to do and/or believe that they might as well be atheists, even if they don't self-identify, like Mr. Jillette certainly does, as such) of not believing in either the fairy tales of the religious or the fairy tales of the Left. I was *fascinated* to see an atheist produce a book defending Christianity ... as it seems a bit like Freud's sarcastic note: *"I can most highly recommend the Gestapo to everyone."*

Cupp's book, Losing Our Religion: The Liberal Media's Attack on Christianity[3] was, strangely, a very uncomfortable read. There obviously are different opinions of what is *dangerous* out there, and Cupp evidently is in the camp that does not see the threat of "Dominionist" Christianity, which is the biggest bogeyman for a *lot* of my friends. The fact that she had *Mike Huckabee* pen a foreword to this indicates that she does not consider strident, unyielding, anti-intellectual, organized religion as a danger, or at least not as much a danger as the Left. Of course, I *agree* that the Left is a threat, and that their shock troops in the MSM have totally perverted what was once a key counter to government over-reach, but painting Christianity as an innocent *victim* of a militant left-wing press creates WAY too much cognitive dissonance for my tastes.

A quote on the dust jacket sets up the tone pretty well:

> *The press has become a political and ideological tool of oppression – politicized, self-aware, self-motivated, and power-hungry ... In short, these people can no longer be trusted.*

Yes, that's true ... but atheist Cupp defending Christianity seems as bizarre to me as Libertarian (and atheist) Jillette defending the Obama regime as being "well meaning"! Frankly, I was never quite able to triangulate where Cupp was coming from here, as she even goes so far to besmirch *the Enlightenment* in her defining a "revolution"

> *If this sounds ominous, it is. And it's much worse than you think.*
>
> ...
>
> *No matter what you believe, and how fervently you believe it, this particular war on God, just the latest in a string of them since the Enlightenment, is a war against <u>all</u> Americans – religious, atheist, and secular – not because of whom it targets, but because of who's behind it.*
>
> ...
>
> *The revolutionaries are in the media.*
>
> *The people you trust to be fair, accurate, objective, and insightful, the so-called watchdogs of the state, protectors of the truth, gatekeepers and guardians of freedom, are the very revolutionaries out to shame, mock, subvert, pervert, corrupt, debase and extinguish your beliefs, the beliefs of the vast majority of Americans, and the values upon which this country was founded. They're doing the one thing they're not supposed to do: They're taking sides. ... this means {the} guardians of truth are being dishonest, wholly subjective, and, frankly, un-American. Targeting faith is targeting Democracy, and that's something that should make every American deeply concerned for the future.*

I'm certainly not going to argue against the concept that the MSM has been *deliberately infiltrated* (along with academia and government) with hard-Left "true believers" (with thrills going up their legs), but I can *not* get how this can be posited to be *more* of a danger than the Dominionist movement, and related groups who seek to create a Biblical theocracy in America.

Anyway, the book is set up with ten "thou shalt" chapters, each focusing on some particular topic of deep interest to both the Leftist MSM and Christian fundamentalists ... all things gay, the bugaboo of evolution, sexual permissiveness, abortion, stem-cell research, etc., etc. ... with Cupp defending the Christian stance in each case. Sure, there is a lot of legitimate finger pointing at the abuses of the media, (things like how blatantly the MSM will blow up a scandal involving a conservative, and totally sweep under the rug equivalent or worse behaviors by liberals) but this *feels* (from where I'm sitting) like defending the kid who killed his parents because he's now an orphan. *Both* sides are vile, yet Cupp doesn't seem to be willing to shine an equivalent light on the similarly dangerous situation of having millions of people out there who believe in religious doctrine over and above science ... or the true underpinnings of our Republic.

Ultimately, the only sense I could make of this was that it was a numbers game ... if you have a media elite that's attacking a "vast majority" of America, it's anti-democracy and bad. Except, come on ... if the beliefs of that majority are preposterous, destructive, and threatening, they *should be mocked*. Cupp certainly makes a lot of valid points about how frustratingly one-sided the Leftist media are, and the deep cynical hypocrisy that goes with that, but she's basically defending the indefensible here ... which is sad.

I had really hoped to have liked Losing Our Religion[4], but – as much as I agreed with her hostility to the MSM – it lacked the balance of highlighting the clear and terrifying hazards of a majority that chooses Bronze Age fairy tales over reason. This is still in print, but the new/used vendors (where I got my copy) at the on-line big boys have it for as little as a penny (plus $3.99 shipping). If this sounds like something you'd want to have a go at ... at least you can get it for cheap!

Notes:

1. http://btripp-books.livejournal.com/154054.html
2. http://en.wikipedia.org/wiki/Russell%27s_teapot
3-4. http://amzn.to/1IE0Jiu

Friday, March 7, 2014[1]

## Absolutely smashing ...

This was a happy discovery at the dollar store ... and just a few weeks ago (it did not languish in the "wall of to-be-read books" like so many do). I know I come off as a cheap bastard, but it makes me so *happy* to get a nice hardcover book for next to nothing ... and especially if it's a book that I actually like (of course, if one of my $1 finds is "meh", I'm also not kicking myself for having spent $25 for it). Obviously a book about the Large Hadron Collider is likely to be pretty current, and the copy I have is from the 2010 first edition (poking around on Amazon, I've found that there is a *revised* reprint edition from 2012 which has been updated with the particulars of the Higgs Boson, discovered 7/4/12).

Of course, this means that Amir D. Aczel's Present at the Creation: the Story of CERN and the Large Hadron Collider[2] (since re-subtitled with "Discovering the Higgs Boson") *is* a bit of a tease since it takes the story up to the point when the LHC is working, but results hadn't come through as yet. Frankly, this was not a smooth process, what was to be the official start of the device was on 09/10/2008, with the counter-rotating proton beams circulating for the first time, but soon after a major problem with the superconducting magnets caused a catastrophic breakdown, which took another 14 months to repair. In November of 2009 they fired it up again, and had the first proton collisions, but it wasn't until 03/30/2010 that it went up to half power (two 3.5 TeV proton beams colliding for a 7 TeV power level) and started to pick apart what was being created.

Aczel has a dozen science books out there, and he obviously knows his stuff. One of the most notable aspects to Present at the Creation[3] is how deftly he handles "setting the stage" for talking about the LHC, as, obviously, there is a LOT of science which needs to get covered to bring the reader up to the point where the project generally makes sense. Needless to say, one *could* spend thousands of pages to get there, but he manages to present (what to me seemed) a decent overview while discussing the development of the LHC ... and he covers a lot: dark matter, anti-matter, superposition, quark theory, black holes, Feynman diagrams, symmetry, fields, etc., etc., etc.

The numbers associated with the LHC are stunning ... it is the largest machine ever constructed, and its detectors (there are a number of separate programs using the same accelerator ring, with the two largest being the CMS, or Compact Muon Solenoid, and the ATLAS) are *huge*, the size of 5-7 story buildings buried deep under the French/Swiss countryside at CERN. When the LHC is pushed to its maximum of 7 TeV per beam, it will be moving those protons at an amazing *99.9999991* percent of the speed of light.

To put that in perspective, if the beam was shot at Alpha Centauri, 4.2 lightyears away from us, it would arrive only 0.3 seconds later than a photon from our Sun (moving, of course, *at* the speed of light). Given that protons are "massive", that 99.9999991 figure is pretty good ... and not likely to be bested any time soon, as, according to relativity, at 100% of the speed of light those protons would achieve infinite mass, which gets messy.

One of the concerns that some had voiced about the LHC was that pushing massive particles that close to infinities might create mini black holes. Aczel discusses a lot of the issues around the worries (including the "theory" that the 2008 melt-down on the magnets was the doing of time travelers from the future trying to prevent the LHC from going on-line!), and admits that there are a lot of things that we can't "know" for sure.

Speaking of the magnets ... unless there is an alien civilization running *bigger* superconducting magnets somewhere out there, the coolant system in the LHC is the *coldest place in the universe*! Most folks are familiar with the idea of "absolute zero" (0 degrees Kelvin, or -459.67° F), but even the empty expanses between galaxies aren't *at* absolute zero, there's a "temperature" of the universe, a leftover from the big bang 13.7 billion years ago, which runs around 2.73 degrees Kelvin, or -454.7° F ... compare that to what the superconducting magnets are cooled to: 1.9 degrees Kelvin, or -456.25° F ... to risk alienating you with a terrible pun ... How COOL is that???

Aczel also covers a number of the other experiments (other than the big two) being developed at the LHC, and discusses details about how a lot of this stuff works. But the book's hardly "technical" (yeah, I know, easy for *me* to say, as I love reading about physics), and deals with a lot of the history of scientific theories and discoveries which led up to the LHC and discusses many of the people involved. I was interested (having a daughter who is about to head off to college to become an engineer) to find that the Coordinator for the ATLAS project (and the 3,000 physicists involved in that part of the LHC!) was a woman, Fabiola Gianotti ... and the list of top Nobel laureates playing parts at CERN is truly impressive.

The scale of the LHC project is mindboggling, if there are *thousands* of *physicists* on board, one can imagine how many engineering specialties are also needed to make these massive machines, and the facilities all along the 17-mile ring of the accelerator, and keep everything running. I must admit to having a twinge of "what could have been" thinking about the US staying the course with the Superconducting Super Collider in north Texas, canceled in 1983 (when it was half done) due to cost over-runs. The SSC would have been bigger (its ring had a 54-mile circumference) and more powerful (at 20 TeV) than the LHC ... and would have been *here*.

As you can tell ... I'm very enthusiastic about Present at the Creation[4], and would highly recommend it to anybody with an interest in physics, or just big amazing projects. As noted, I found this at the dollar store a month or so back, so $1 copies are kicking around out there, but I'd recommend getting the*new* edition (the 2012 paperback) with the Higgs info in it. It's reasonably priced, and, of course, the on-line big boys have it at a discount, and you can save a bit via the new/used channels (but it seems that the hardcover is the older version, so keep that in mind).

Notes:

1. http://btripp-books.livejournal.com/154135.html

2-4. http://amzn.to/1HjLEj2

Saturday, April 5, 2014[1]

# This may BE your grandfather's freaky ...

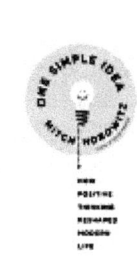

This is another book from the LibraryThing.com "Early Reviewer" program, and the second time that I've received multiples of a particular author's books (I reviewed Occult America[2] back in 2009). This new one by Mitch Horowitz, One Simple Idea: How Positive Thinking Reshaped Modern Life[3] is just a few degrees off from his previous, but this time looking at the development of the "positive thinking" (*"The Secret"*[4] "law of attraction") stuff that has been such a cultural feature over the past decade.

Now, given that I have at least two ancestors who came over on the Mayflower (my late Aunt, who was very active in the Mayflower Society, somehow managed to have one more than the rest of us), I can say this ... but is it *really* a surprise that in a country initiated by religious whackjobs there has been a whole chain of "out of the box" thinking in that wookie-wookie zone? If you look at it from that perspective, no ... but being the sort who might otherwise out-of-hand dismiss a lot of the "newage" as being rooted in people who damaged their brains in the 1960's, it's amazing how long a lot of this stuff has been around.

Like in his previous book, Horowitz takes a historical approach to this, backgrounding it with early aspects as far back as Greek-Egyptian Hermeticism, through the Idealists, Kant and Hegel, the Modernists, Schopenhauer and Nietzsche, and into Swedenborg and Emerson, as counterparts to America's dour Calvinist Protestantism. The story picks up in the 1830's with a fellow by the name of Quimby who encounters traveling students of Mesmer, first Poyen, and then Collyer. Quimby began healing, writing, and building a following, including, in the mid-1860's a young lady who would become Mary Baker Eddy, the founder of the Christian Science movement.

Frankly, this is the point where it starts to be difficult to give a running commentary, as the players, publications, and groups start weaving their paths through the culture, and there are (as one can get a sense of in the previous paragraph) a *lot* of names which may or may not strike the reader with particular significance. Horowitz does an admirable job of keeping this moving forward without too much confusion, blocking out the book into thematic, albeit still reasonably chronological, chapters, looking at how these groups cross-pollinated through the decades.

Familiar names keep popping up, if in not particularly familiar contexts, and there seems to be always a mystical/occult extreme that many of these groups were informed by, but avoided in an effort to maintain a "Christian" facade. While many drew on Swedenborg, more than a few were at least conversant with Blavatsky and the Theosophists. I was surprised to read that things like "New Thought" and "Prosperity Gospel" were not just hippie-era spins, but dated back to the 1920's. The rise of psychotherapy also has its influence, with Freud, Jung, and others either being inspirations for insights or trends to be countered.

Each chapter is subdivided in sections dealing with individuals and their circles, showing how they were inter-related (some being outright schismatic, some having paths that crossed, melded, split, etc.) with other figures in the general thematic flow of the chapter. In the course of this, whole constellations of related (if not *involved*) figures, from Susan B. Anthony to J.B. Rhine and even Carlos Castaneda and Ronald Reagan (some *fascinating* stuff about him!) appear. Of course, all the "big names" are here, Napoleon Hill, Dale Carnegie, Norman Vincent Peale, etc., etc., etc., with looks at where their concepts arose, and how they influenced others.

Again, the names just keep coming … somebody better read in this particular niche would no doubt recognize dozens (possibly *hundreds*), but as the book progresses, they become more and more familiar, with people either still around in the "inspirational" fields or deceased only in the past few decades. Of course, Horowitz works his way up to *The Secret* but doesn't try to survey the wide expanse of "practitioners" that spawned. The story, however, continues, even up to difficulties that the Tony Robbins organization was having as recently as 2012.

The final chapter of One Simple Idea[5] is called (tellingly) "Does It Work?" where he pulls together the historical bits and tries to define "the lay of the land", in which he posits that there are four basic "schools" into which most of these people and movements can be sorted:

1. The Magical Thinking or Divine Thought School
2. The Conditioning or Reprogramming School
3. The Conversion School
4. The Meaning-Based School

These are interesting, but not pressed too hard; he discusses these as *tendencies* of various groups, but avoids being overly specific as to which practitioners are in which "school". He follows this with a look at the "scientific" side of things, from the no doubt very applicable "placebo effect" to the far less concrete, albeit very popular, attempts to bend quantum physics to mystical ends. In closing, Horowitz notes:

> *The pioneers of the positive-thinking movement, acting with deep practical intent, probed the possibilities and capacities of our psyches earlier than any scientists, theologians, or psychologists of the modern industrial age. The founders of New Thought and affirmative thinking created a fresh means of viewing life, one that was rough and incomplete, rife with mistakes and dead ends, but also filled with possibility and practical application.*

While I'm not sure if a hard-core "The Secret" believer would particularly appreciate One Simple Idea[6] (as it's pretty well-grounded in reality), it certainly has a lot to recommend it to those who have encountered that sort of belief and wondered where the heck it came from. Horowitz has succeeded in wrapping a reasonably coherent story arc across a vast lot of individual story lines, which makes this much more than a string of Wikipedia pages on the persons and groups involved. If you have an interest in things in this realm, you will likely find a lot of useful info (if nothing else, a vast number of books to check out!) here. This is brand new, just out in January, so you're likely to be able to find it in your local real-world book vendor, but you could save a few bucks with the on-line guys if you're in one of those "bereft of bookstores" zones.

Notes:

1. http://btripp-books.livejournal.com/154464.html
2. http://btripp-books.livejournal.com/81115.html
3. http://amzn.to/1HjLbNF
4. http://btripp-books.livejournal.com/33791.html
5-6. http://amzn.to/1HjLbNF

Sunday, April 6, 2014[1]

# Quite Revealing ...

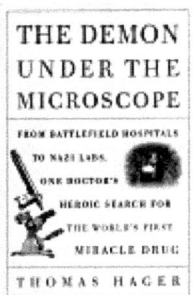

Here is another of those wonderful dollar store finds that lend an element of serendipity to my reading. Frankly, this one had sat around for a very long time, waiting for me "to get in the right place" for a medically-themed historic survey ... but after quite a number of business books, I needed a break, and this seemed to be variable enough to be "next".

I'm somewhat embarrassed that it took me until about half-way through the book to think "you know, this is really just about this one guy!", where, had I paid closer attention to the subtitle of Thomas Hager's The Demon Under the Microscope: From Battlefield Hospitals to Nazi Labs, One Doctor's Heroic Search for the World's First Miracle Drug[2], I'd have possibly noted the "One Doctor's" part. Instead, I launched into this thinking it was a general overview of the development of antibiotics.

Of course, the book *is* about the development of antibiotics, and it's pretty amazing to realize just how recent these have come along. I was familiar with the story of Ignaz Semmelweis, a Hungarian doctor who in the 1850's introduced the idea of *antiseptics* to a medical community that really didn't want to hear it (at that time, surgeons wore their bloody smocks, patient to patient, as something as a badge of honor), but he, at one hospital in Vienna, was able to reverse the numbers which had *three times* the deaths of mothers in obstetric wards staffed by *doctors* verses those being run by *midwives*, eventually pushing mortality rates to under 1% of patients. Since there was no "germ theory" at the time, and despite his successes, Semmelweis was decreed to be mad and died in an asylum!

The Demon Under the Microscope[3], however, primarily follows the work of Gerhard Domagk, who had been a medical student prior to WWI, volunteered for the German army, was wounded, and served the rest of the war as a medic. The book goes into a great deal of detail about how most deaths in WWI came not from initial damage from gunshots, shrapnel, etc., but from the infections following. While by this time the use of antiseptics had become accepted (although hard to maintain on the battlefield), there still wasn't much that could be done. Diseases, especially the dreaded Streptococcus, would quickly do in those with any but the most minor injuries.

As most folks reading this will understand, this came as a bit of a shock. In the West, in the past half century, "strep" is a bothersome throat infection that will occasionally run through a school, but be quickly put down with antibiotics ... it's something one gets one's kids tested for if they have a throat infection ... but it's never been something that I had any idea was so horribly *lethal*. And yet, in the years before the Second World War, it was pretty much a death sentence, and a strep infection could take a young, otherwise healthy, person in a matter of days. Hager notes:

> *Strep might seem an odd choice today when the only strep disease most people ever experience is a bad sore throat. In the 1920s, however, it was one of the most feared killers on earth. No one was safe from strep.*

To illustrate this point he walks the reader through the sad tale of Calvin Coolidge Jr., who was a teen in his father's White House. One day he went out and played tennis in sneakers without socks, and got a blister on his toe … two days later he was weak and feverish, a couple of more days later he was transferred to Walter Reed Hospital, being attended by the finest physicians, and, a week after getting the blister, the boy was dead.

A dozen years later, another Presidential son, Franklin Delano Roosevelt Jr., fell ill with a sinus infection, which turned into a fast-spreading strep infection. Near to death, his family approves the use of a brand new drug out of Europe … Sulfa-based drugs from Bayer … and the patient had a fast, full, and nearly miraculous recovery.

The sulfa drugs were discovered by Domagk and his predecessors almost by accident. Most of their research followed the discovery that certain dyes had properties that stopped certain diseases (first discovered when using dyes for staining slides) … with an early success being an azo dye that cured "sleeping sickness", a significant threat to the European colonial powers in Africa. Once this initial drug was on the market, the dye manufactures launched research programs with their chemists creating molecule after molecule that would form the basis of tests on animals that had been infected with a number of diseases. At one point a sulfa compound had been added to a dye and they suddenly saw remarkable survival rates in their strep test animals. As it turned out, the sulfa was the key ingredient (much to Bayer's dismay, as it was cheap, easy to manufacture, and not patentable like their dye-based products).

Of course, in the 20's and 30's, drugs were hardly controlled, and there was a *long* history of "patent medicines":

> *Patent medicines in the early part of the twentieth century were as firmly established a part of American culture as jazz or baseball. Americans were accustomed to medicating themselves, deciding on their own treatments, and buying their own drugs. It went against the grain to have some doctor or federal agency telling Americans how to cure themselves.*

Unfortunately, once the idea of sulfa caught on in the US, there were hundreds of companies making products based on this, including one, Massengill, which produced an "elixir" that was sweet, raspberry flavored, and based on the industrial solvent diethyline glycol – a substance sometime used in salves and lotions – one of the few things in which the sulfa compounds would dissolve. Very quickly after its introduction, reports of deaths started to come in, from kids taking it for sore throats to folks trying to treat VD, they were drinking the "elixir" and dropping dead. The government and medical establishment quickly tried to halt distribution, but over a hundred people had died. This was not "good press", and many people suspected the "new German drug" sulfa, rather than the toxic delivery system.

The coming of WW2 was, however, the heyday for sufla, and it ended up being in the personal kits of most of the allied soldiers, causing many fewer post-engagement casualties than in any previous war, but it was also quickly eclipsed by the development of penicillin in the late 30's. Domagk had been awarded the Nobel Prize for his work in 1939, but had been prevented from accepting it by the Nazi regime, yet he survived the war, and was able to receive the honor afterwards.

The Demon Under the Microscope[4] is an engaging read, and a real eye-opener (as noted) at how *recent* much of the medical resources we have today were developed. It is part medical history, part military history, and an interesting look at how haphazard much of scientific advances are, frequently coming from something that wasn't being specifically looked for, but arising out of fortuitous accidents. The edition I have is the 2006 hardback, found at the dollar store, and there is a more recent paperback version as well ... which appears to be the only one actually in print at this point. The online big boys have the paperback at a bit off its very reasonable cover price, but the new/used guys have copies of the hardcover for as little as 1¢ (plus shipping). If you have an interest in the various types of history that pull together here, or of medical stuff in general, you'll probably enjoy this, and given how reasonable it would be to score a copy, I'd recommend you take a chance on it.

Notes:

1. http://btripp-books.livejournal.com/154833.html

2-4. http://amzn.to/1EpBfQF

Thursday, May 1, 2014[1]

# Letting your freak flag fly ...

So, regular readers of this space will recognize Chris Brogan as a frequent author reviewed here. I think I've covered all his books over the years (Social Media 101[2], Trust Agents[3], Google+ for Business[4], and The Impact Equation[5]), and had the opportunity to get a pre-publication copy of his newest, The Freaks Shall Inherit the Earth: Entrepreneurship for Weirdos, Misfits, and World Dominators[6], in plastic-bound "galleys" from the good folks at Wiley.

As Chris notes at one point: this is *not* a book about Social Media (his generally-acknowledged "niche"). Rather, it's a look at how those of us who are not cookie-cutter clones seeking the paycheck-producing sanctuary of the corporate cubical *{cue the Leonard Cohen music[7]: "But you see that line there moving through the station? / I told you, I told you, told you, I was one of those"}* can find ways to succeed, thrive, and even *dominate* in the chaos of this changing world.

Of course, this is not a new vision ... the underpinnings of Brogan's thesis rest on (if not necessarily arise from) many recent manifestos, from Timothy Ferriss' 4-Hour Workweek[8] to Seth Godin's Tribes[9], and the like ... the difference being that in Freaks[10], a particular sub-set of the population is addressed, those who in a different time might have found less hope for succeeding in business.

Who are the "freaks" the book deals with? The Preface starts out with a look at the upcoming *Guardians of the Galaxy* movie that Marvel/Disney is putting out, and how unlikely a subject that is for something that costs millions to make and requires hundreds of approvals from a certified Big Business entity. Brogan adds:

> The freaks already have inherited the earth, my friend. Weirdos and misfits are now the world dominators. It used to be that all the crazy fringe interests of the world were absolutely underground. Now, the underground has become the core of a thriving and somewhat hard-to-track new economy. Trends have a hard time covering this stuff, unless we start squinting.
>
> That jobless recovery? Where are all those people going? I'll tell you one group of people who aren't rushing back to their cubicles: freaks. Instead, they're becoming artisan pickle makers in Brooklyn, punk rock dog groomers in Memphis, and zombie apocalypse race organizers in Boston.
> ...

His timing for one example job ... "YouTube Celebrity" ... couldn't be better, coming right when Google's video arm is saturating the Chicago subway cars with pictures[11] of young ladies whose cupcake-baking, fashion, and make-up advice clips have netted *millions* of subscribers (and ad revenue checks in the six to seven figure range!).

Obviously, most of the "freaks" aren't into those lofty financial neighborhoods, but the possibilities are out there (in reading this I couldn't help but think of the "freak flag flying" style exhibited by Salvador Dali ... in a far less freak-friendly age). The book, however, is structured to be a guide for making a success from whatever one's unconventional passions are. Chris takes it from the most basic: *"A company's goal is to sell <u>something of value to a buyer</u>. It exists to offer a service or product for some kind of payment. Simple, right?"* ... and then starts to break things down to what you'll need to face/know/accept in the process of making that work for you.

The middle chapters are aimed at particular types of business, from the "employeepreneur" to those who are running fairly sizable businesses (he even floats Marissa Mayer as a potential "freak" running Yahoo), and he suggests that readers go ahead and skip those sections that don't seem to be what they're dealing with. However, these are predicated on some core material ... defining success ... building skills ... setting goals ... structuring your days ... and what I found particularly interesting (being one of those guys who's not comfortable without all the details mapped out in advance) "Fall in Love with Not Knowing", which reminded me of the teachings of a Korean Zen master I once heard.

Once the groundwork is set, and one has been "sorted" as to the type of business one's in, the real "meat" of the book comes in. Returning to the "not knowing" theme, he posits that "you have to know only enough to start" (a more palatable stance than Ferriss' view of "expertise" being that one only has to *"know more about the topic than the purchaser"*), specialization vs. being a generalist, and dealing with the fear of failure. On this last point he states: *"My success is built entirely on my ability to fail quickly and then learn and adapt from the results of that failure."* while presenting a 7-point "battle plan" for preparing for and dealing with failure ... and then goes into a whole chapter on "obstacles and challenges".

I found the following three chapters most useful, "Build Your Own Media Empire", "Connect with Your Freaks", and "Own Everything" ... each of which is full of examples, instructions, etc. ... with the latter being about responsibility rather than acquisition. One of the characters who pops up here and there in the book is famed skateboarder Tony Hawk, and in this context he talks about how Hawk went against pretty much everybody to provide an affordable board with his name on it, getting flak from some saying he was "selling out" and from others who couldn't imagine selling a quality board at the price point he was envisioning. The book is full of glimpses at various characters and ventures ... from the UFC becoming huge because they "told the story better" to his son, whose "Creeper" (from Minecraft) Halloween costume formed its own "community".

Brogan, of course, is no Pollyanna, blind to the sobering realities of how frequently businesses fail, so the penultimate chapter is about "When It All Goes Wrong", looking at approaches and strategies for when things fail. One of the more interesting things here is sort of an "entrepreneur's hierarchy of needs" to fall back on when things go bad. He's also fairly adamant about taking responsibility when things have gone bad through your own screw-ups, and sketches out his recommendations on how to deal with that.

Finally, there's a chapter about taking action. No doubt there are even more businesses that don't get started than those that fail ... and you won't have the learning experiences of failure (let alone "the thrill of victory" from starting a successful business) if that idea of yours just stays comfortably tucked between the folds of your cerebrum. A 12-step plan (generally following the chapters of the book) is presented here to walk the reader through how to go from accepting your Freakhood to dominating the world.

The Freaks Shall Inherit the Earth[12] is new just last week, so should be nice and shiny in those few remaining brick-and-mortar book retailers. Of course, the on-line big boys have it, and at a fairly steep discount (at this writing, 36% off the cover price). This is a pretty awesome look at the possibilities of creating your own business, but one that's still realistic about the pitfalls and challenges along that path. If you've ever had an inclination to take your personal quirks and make a career of them, you'll want to pick up a copy of this!

Notes:

1. http://btripp-books.livejournal.com/155126.html
2. http://btripp-books.livejournal.com/90703.html
3. http://btripp-books.livejournal.com/89349.html
4. http://btripp-books.livejournal.com/124374.html
5. http://btripp-books.livejournal.com/136831.html
6. http://amzn.to/1KZDjmY
7. http://www.azlyrics.com/lyrics/leonardcohen/firstwetakemanhattan.html
8. http://btripp-books.livejournal.com/93466.html
9. http://btripp-books.livejournal.com/104230.html
10. http://amzn.to/1KZDjmY
11. http://adage.com/article/special-report-tv-upfront/youtube-run-tv-ads-promoting-creators-big-2014-push/292468/
12. http://amzn.to/1KZDjmY

Saturday, May 10, 2014[1]

# The evolution of MarComm ...

This was another book that I made a special request to the publisher for a copy, and was kindly sent one from the good folks over at QUE. As regular readers of this space (who'd read my earlier review of her Marketing in the Round[2]) may recall, I know Gini Dietrich (who's the CEO of the Arment Dietrich "integrated marketing communications" firm) from the local Social Media scene ... as well as from a particular corner of Facebook occupied by notable marketing maniacs. So, *of course*, I needed to get her new book, Spin Sucks: Communication and Reputation Management in the Digital Age[3], in for review!

Now, if "Spin Sucks" sounds familiar, it's also the name of her site offering "Professional Development for PR and Marketing Pros", which is the home[4] of her noted "Gin and Topics" blog. This book shares something with the aim of her site, as it reads to me as primarily targeted at *established* PR/Marketing types (like myself, who grew up in a PR family back in the "Mad Men" days, and has been kicking around MarCom ever since I could shave), rather than being a manifesto of "something new" (like her previous book was), presenting an overview of the PR discipline over time, and showing how it's evolving.

In fact, in the Introduction, after tracing the predecessors of PR to the Babylonians, the Counter-Reformation (when the term "propaganda" was coined by the Vatican), and through Freud to his cigarette-marketing nephew, she notes:

> If you run an organization, are on an executive team, or have (or need to have) communications professionals or a firm reporting to you, this book will show you how to prepare your business for a marathon instead of a sprint, how to build a communications program that ... will deliver more valuable long-lasting results, as well as a spotless reputation. You'll also learn how the lines between marketing, advertising, digital, and PR are blurring ...

The book (which is rather *concise* at under 150 pages) is broken into four thematic sections: "Tell Your Story Without Sex or Extortion", "Scammers, Liars, and Beggars", "Your Brand; Your Customers", and the titular "Spin Sucks". One of the most appealing aspects of Gini's books is that she's writing "from the trenches", and her advice typically comes with concrete examples of when things were done right and done wrong. The start of the "story telling" part features the words of Larry Brooks: *"An 'idea' is not inherently a concept."* which then unfolds into the idea of dramatic presentation, with five essential parts: *passion, a protagonist, an antagonist, a revelation, and a transformation* (which, admittedly, *does* sound like a fairly big reach for presenting "your organization's story", but that's what you're going to want to end up telling).

The next section deals with things you do *not* want to do ... especially in relation to your content's interaction with Google. She walks the reader though many iterations of the Google algorithm, what folks did to "game" the system, and of how even major corporations got on the wrong side of Google bans. Obviously, this is a "moving target", but she presents a list of 15 questions to ask yourself that should end up getting you on the right side of the algorithms, which she notes pretty much boils down to: *"If you don't want to bookmark it and share it, no one else will, either."*

Dietrich moves into defining what is currently "shareable and valuable" content, setting up a framework of four types of media: Paid, Earned, Shared, and Owned ... with a somewhat confusing Venn diagram (some intersections have no tags, some have multiple), with 8 categories and a few dozen items, and "Authority" being at the center of the four circles. To give a sense of how the different types of media inter-relate, she discusses a DirectTV promotion, which involved a music video-like production featuring the NFL's Manning family, that never aired, but went to YouTube and their own site. She notes: *"They used paid (because it cost them money to produce it), owned media (it is embedded both on their website and their YouTube channel), and shared media for this campaign, and earned media is the result."* ... with there being a *half a million* <u>news</u> results in Google for the spot – meaning that nearly that number of media outlets picked up the spot and included in their content. That's some serious "earnings".

She then works to define each of these four categories, and talks of things to do and to avoid in each, and moves into examples of building community, generating leads, and driving sales. One thing she goes into depth on is using a webinar to generate leads, with a 14-point action plan on how to set that up ... with the suggestion to *"not wait until you can afford enterprise-level software, but use what is available to you now in an effective way."* Dietrich then comes up with 25 resources and methods to help come up with good content ... some of these are amazing, and some of these are simply thinking about other things (you're probably already doing) in a new way ... and then closes out the first section with a review of the hoary news release, and "best practices" for doing on-line versions of this.

The numbered "action lists" that Gini has throughout the book are very useful, and are certainly one of the highlights here. Again, you can tell that these are coming from hard-fought experience and not some off-the-top-of-the-head "ivory tower" pontificating. The second section is full of good advice on how to deal with hostile reactions to your sites and other materials, how the unscrupulous attempt to control the media, and what happens with all those "black hat" practitioners out there. There are many fascinating stories of companies who ran afoul of these hazards, and how they fought back, plus a great deal of good step-by-step advice for handling different situations along these lines.

The third section has just one chapter: Your Customers Control the Brand ... which is probably one of the hardest lessons to get through to the traditional MBA marketer. One sub-heading here says *"Your Brand Is How Customers Feel About You"*, which puts control out of the hands of the ad guys, and into the end user – and their Social network:

> In today's 24/7/365 digital world, brand development happens constantly. It's an ongoing two-way conversation between an organization and its customers. You introduce new products or services and begin the conversation. Your customers respond and react – sometimes very vocally and sometimes more quietly. You respond and refine based on what they're saying.

Of course, this brings in the question of *how* to listen to and involve your customers, and various approaches are dissected to come up with the best approaches for one's specific business.

Finally, there's the Spin Sucks section, where more history is detailed, and a few things (such as on-page SEO) are specifically looked at. There's a chapter on crisis communications, and the steps necessary to ride out the rough spots ... along with examples of when things went *very* wrong for various companies, and how they dealt with that. The book closes with a look ahead, touching on everything from self-driving cars to predictions that: *"The lines between communications, marketing, advertising, sales, customer experience, product development, and human resources will become so blurred it will be hard to decipher where each belongs."*

I really enjoyed Spin Sucks[5], and got quite a lot out of it (I found, while writing this, that most of my little bookmarks were on things for my own "future reference" rather than stuff for the review!). As it just came out in March, it will no doubt be available in the brick-and-mortar places with good business sections, but the on-line Big Boys are offering it in both paperback and e-book formats at a discount. Obviously, this isn't something for *everybody*, but if you have an interest in marketing, PR, and how business in general is having to adapt to the tech realities of today and tomorrow, this will likely be something you'll find of value.

Notes:

1. http://btripp-books.livejournal.com/155380.html
2. http://btripp-books.livejournal.com/149388.html
3. http://amzn.to/1Jc0AOX
4. http://spinsucks.com/
5. http://amzn.to/1Jc0AOX

Monday, May 12, 2014[1]

# Another green read ...

As regular readers of this space know, I've often been "confused" when books that I've picked up at the dollar store have been sitting over on Amazon at full price. Well, this one is *clearly* a "dollar store buy" that's out of print (and hardcover copies available for very little). This may be due to it being a bit "old" (it came out in February of 2006) and much of the specific info (politically, etc.) being out of date at this point.

That said, I found Josh Tickell's Biodiesel America: How to Achieve Energy Security, Free America from Middle-east Oil Dependence And Make Money Growing Fuel[2] a very informative read, which filled in the details on a lot of the background on this "green tech" fuel.

Obviously, the parts which were "historical" at the time of the book's writing are, perhaps, the most useful, as they remain constant, while a lot of the "current info" in the book is well into the rear-view mirror. Among the subjects covered is a very interesting look at Diesel in general, how it was developed, spread, and became a niche product in the U.S. vs. its acceptance elsewhere in the world (at the time of writing, some EU countries had as much as 65% diesel penetration). This is, of course, framed in the context of the American oil industry, and the author paints a *very* grim picture of both U.S. and global oil supplies ... frankly, from his "the sky is falling" prognostications, I'm surprised that more of this hasn't been daily headline material, as this presents an immediate threat, eight years ago ... perhaps nobody is talking about key Saudi oil fields failing, or maybe the emergency that Tickell outlines was a bit over-blown.

There are several interesting sections here, breaking down the various elements of assorted factors of the energy industry – largely set out in chapter called "Alternative Fuels 101". Among the highlights of this are the following lists:

> The Three Principles of Good Energy:
>   I. Energy Balance Ratio
>   II. The Cost of Externalities
>   III. Ease of Integration with Existing Infrastructure
>
> Six Engines that Move Our World:
>   I. Gasoline
>   II. Diesel
>   III. Electric
>   IV. Gasoline-Electric Hybrids
>   V. Diesel-Electric Hybrids
>   VI. The Air Car

*The Fossil-Based Alternatives:*
   *I. Natural Gas (Methane)*
   *II. Liquified Natural Gas (NLG)*
   *III. Propane (LPG – Liquified Petroleum Gas)*
   *IV. Methanol*
   *V. Hydrogen*
   *VI. Gas to Liquid Fuel (GTL) or Fischer Tropsch (FT)*

*The Renewables:*
   *I. Biomass*
   *II. Methane (from digestion)*
   *III. Ethanol*
   *IV. Biodiesel*

*Alternative Electricity:*
   *I. Nuclear*
   *II. Geothermal*
   *III. Hydro*
   *IV. Solar*
   *V. Wind*

Each of these is discussed (in varying detail), with many fascinating data points, such as *"In an area equivalent to a 45-mile radius (6,600 square miles), the United States could produce 100% of its daily 10 billion kilowatt hours electricity demand using photovoltaic panels."* - this accompanied by a map of the U.S. with a fairly small black circle on the California-Nevada border.

After this the book swings into the politics and business of farming, the info here no doubt being somewhat stale by now, as a lot of stuff that's being featured here has either worked itself out (NAFTA, GATT), or have been likely superseded by other legislation. What's particularly interesting in this chapter is a look at various crops and their applicability to fuel. These are Soybeans (of which the U.S. Produces 45% of the world's crop), Rapeseed & Canola (which are widely grown in Northern Europe), Mustard, Peanut, Sunflower, and Corn (Maize). Of these the most fascinating was Mustard ... which I'd not heard of before as a potential fuel source. The seed is between 25% and 40% oil by weight, and has very high yields. A Department of Energy report outlines 14 criteria for potential oil crops, and Mustard fits all of them ... including the ability (in #1) to "supply 6-12 billion gallons of feedstock oil". It struck me that the plant can be used for both human and animal food ("mustard greens"), that having wide-spread production would be useful for both that and fuel. Another intriguing possibility is Algae, the type studied for this being approximately 50% oil by weight. However, here are some serious complications on how to efficiently grow Algae in sufficiently large scale (as it needs both a lot of water and sunlight, and typically a place that has plenty one is pretty short on the other).

The next chapter deals with Biodiesel itself, going back to Rudolf Diesel's experiments with various vegetable oils to run his engines. Interest in this fuel source had a spike in the oil crisis of the 1970s, but the bulk of the research on it, in the U.S. at least, has only been since the 90's. The author goes into the chemistry of producing Biodiesel, and looks at various aspects of it in relation to other fuels, from efficiency in the engine to the sorts of air pollution it may produce. He also looks at challenges to its use, including its viscosity in cold condition, its tendency to degrade rubber parts, and its slow acceptance in terms of engine warranty rules.

After this the book turns to the efforts to get Biodiesel accepted in various levels of the government ... and how many locations – even despite it costing significantly more than standard fuels – have switched their vehicle fleets to using some portion of Biodiesl fuel. The author is evidently quite enthused about this, but the data from a decade ago is not terribly pertinent today. He does take a look at how Biodiesel could be integrated into the existing fuel distribution channels ... how big to make plants, where to locate them, how to transport it, etc., which are no doubt questions that still need to have answers. An interesting angle is that of "National Energy Security": *"... it is not just our dependence on foreign oil, but our dependence on oil itself, that puts the United States in a vulnerable position."*

Biodiesel America[3] has an *extensive* bibliography, running 16 pages of listings, so there's plenty of stuff there to follow up on, and there are endnotes which largely focus on giving the source materials for the assorted referenced materials (such as the DOE report noted above). If you are interested in learning more about Biodiesel, this might be a good place to start. It's a fascinating read, made a bit uneven by the "dated" nature of much of the political/trend material. While it does appear to be out of print, the on-line guys have it for as little as a penny (plus shipping) for a used copy, and 15¢ for a new one ... so it won't cost you much to get it.

Notes:

1. http://btripp-books.livejournal.com/155603.html

2-3. http://amzn.to/1xwrVpz

Saturday, May 17, 2014[1]

# Say you're the CEO of a large corporation ...

Excuse me if I start off this review with a particularly convoluted contemplation of stuff, only particularly related to the book at hand. This was another title that came to me via the LibraryThing.com "Early Reviewer" program. In this program, publishers make a certain number of copies (often 15-25, sometimes more, occasionally less) available of titles they're promoting, and there are usually a hundred or so titles in play. LT members can click a button to "request" a book, and there isn't any limit (that I'm aware of) to how many requests they can put it ... but, generally speaking (there are occasional exceptions), each user can only get *one* book each month. Matching the books to the readers is done by a computer program, known around LT as "The Almighty Algorithm", which looks at info on the book, and the requesting member's book collection. Obviously, if one only requested a single book that one really really wanted, one is at the mercy of said algorithm, and if it doesn't consider your library the 15th (or however many copies are available) best match for the book, you're out of luck. So, it "pays" to request a handful of books each month.

Now, as somebody who doesn't read fiction, the plausible options for me in any given month are somewhat thin, so I find myself frequently "requesting" books that only "sound vaguely interesting" and are certainly NOT things that I would have "free range" ever picked up at a bookstore or ordered online.

As regular readers of this space will appreciate, I have been reading and reviewing a LOT of "business books" over the past several years, but I really had *never* touched one before getting a (free) copy of Conor Cunneen's *"Why Ireland Never Invaded America"* at a lecture he was giving back in 2006. This really didn't open up any floodgates, but it did prime me for doing more business books, which started to come my way when I took over writing *The Job Stalker* on the Tribune's Chicago Now blogging site in 2009. In developing content for that blog, I read and reviewed dozens of "job search" books, and started building relationships with the promotion departments of several of the business publishers.

So, over those years, the complexion of my library changed, and was more and more "business-oriented" which only intensified with my delving (for professional reasons) into the Social Media and Marketing niches. And ... this was data upon which "The Almighty Algorithm" was basing its decisions. In a month that I might have requested a biography, a history book, a philosophical treatise, a pop culture memoir, *and* a business book, the odds started to seriously skew towards the latter. Since (it seems to me) the vast majority of other LT members participating in the Early Reviewers program were looking for fiction, or less serious subjects, my having all those business books in my library made it almost a given that if I requested one (even if it was my 5th choice – there's no system of ranking preferences), I was pretty much a lock for getting it.

Which brings me (500 words in) to the book in question, which would have been highly unlikely to have ever made it into my "to be read" piles without the invisible hand of LT's "Almighty Algorithm". Neil Smith's How Excellent Companies Avoid Dumb Things: Breaking the 8 Hidden Barriers that Plague Even the Best Businesses[2] is, despite the extensive caveats above, a reasonably engaging read, but it's one of those books that is really for bigger businesses than I've ever worked in (well, I've had *clients* like that in my PR days ... but he notes his system has been *"used in companies that have tens of thousands of employees and many divisions, as well in smaller, less complex organizations with fewer than 3,000 employees"* - and that is pretty huge even on the lower end), which made it difficult for me to connect with the info on a truly meaningful level.

A sure sign of this was that I got through the entire book without placing *any* of the little bookmarks I put in to get back to places with either choice quotes for these reviews, or hot tips that I could personally use, until two right towards the end of the book. Yet, the book did not *drag*, it was a reasonably easy read, with interesting stuff, that would no doubt be excellent to the bigger-business folks that are the author's clients. Oh, and that was another bit of a sticking point ... I've chastised other authors for writing "long-form promotional brochures" for their business, and Neil Smith keeps returning again and again to name-checking his consulting product - "The PGI Promise®" (yes, with the ® every time it's mentioned), which is his company's name, Promontory Growth and Innovation, paired with the acronym for his system: "A Promise". Regular readers know what I think of most of these acronyms ... but here's what his stands for (the "Eight Barriers") ...

> **A**voiding Controversy
> **P**oor Use of Time
> **R**eluctance to Change
> **O**rganizational Silos
> **M**anagement Blockers
> **I**ncorrect Information and Bad Assumptions
> **S**ize Matters
> **E**xisting Processes

These are also the subjects of the first eight chapters in the book. What keeps this readable (and even entertaining) is that the author makes this personal, doing set-ups for chapters out of his experience (a story about driving through Nebraska to introduce "Silos"), and tossing out a handful of interesting case studies about how the "Barrier" in question posed problems for a particular company ... in the case of "Organizational Silos", how an insurance company's Sales and Technology departments were working at counter purposes, and costing the company money, how a moving company couldn't figure out why, out of all things they shipped, the dining room tables were getting damaged, and how a food manufacturer ended up using

30 different chocolates in its products, with nearly as many sources, and each product group clutching to their particular recipes (they ended up finding they could do with just *eight* once things were being looked at across the entire company). In each chapter he then has sections called "Baring the Barrier" where he looks at the "how and why" that situation arises and "Breaking the Barrier" with his general game plan for moving past it. Another interesting piece that's in some chapters (but not all – and I thought this was a mistake, it would have been much better to have this as a piece of the consideration of each "Barrier") is a psychological look at the nature of that behavior, by a Dr. Richard Levak.

After the 8 "Barriers" are considered, there is a chapter with "The 12 Principles for Breaking Barriers" - which is pretty much the author's "game plan" with very specific action points and rules to follow (you can find them on p.10 of this sample PDF[3] from the publisher), if being very corporate and HR-y. In this he describes how to make these changes happen (which is not always a pretty sight). This is followed by another look at the psychological aspects, including the potentially painful in recognition "Twenty Reasons for Killing Good Ideas".

The program is then walked through in "A 100-Day Process for Breaking Barriers", which lays the groundwork for the over-all effort in which *"All ideas must be implemented within 36 months; 60 to 70 percent will be implemented within the first year."*. It's Big, it's Corporate, and this chapter is rife with acronyms for various point positions, committees, and work groups. Not my favorite part of the book ... but it's where the process is laid out. Smith closes with a look at the results that one (assuming that one is the head of a huge company) can expect from all this ... he cites a 25% average increase in profits, and quotes "satisfied customers" who say stuff like *"I would have done this process even if there was no significant financial gain."*

Needless to say, How Excellent Companies Avoid Dumb Things[4] isn't for everybody. As interesting a read as it manages to be, it's still targeted to a very narrow market, and most of it isn't particularly "actionable" unless you're in that elevated niche. This didn't stop its hardcover edition from becoming a "New York Times Bestseller", so there were a lot of people reading it, and I guess the "early" aspect of this being in the "Early Reviewers" program is that it's in paperback now. I suppose that this *will* be in the business-oriented brick-and-mortar stores, but at the moment the on-line big boys have it at a whopping 60% off of cover ... and the new/used guys have "very good" copies of the paperback for as little as a penny (plus the $3.99 shipping, of course). For this being something that I probably wouldn't have picked up at the Dollar Store, it was a good read, but I'm not sure if I (not being the head of a 20,000 employee corporation) got much useable out of it, but maybe you might.

Notes:

1. http://btripp-books.livejournal.com/155741.html
2. http://amzn.to/1J6wChe
3. http://www.palgrave.com/PDFs/9781137003065.pdf
4. http://amzn.to/1J6wChe

Sunday, May 18, 2014[1]

# Escaping the old paradigm's cage ...

I had wanted to read this one ever since it came out. Unfortunately, as is frequently the case with his books, Seth Godin's The Icarus Deception: How High Will You Fly?[2] spent a *very* long time hovering right around cover price, even in the new/used channels, and in my seemingly-unending "income challenged" state, I'd just not been able to justify pulling the trigger on it. Fortunately, I caught a "like new" copy for a "reasonable" amount (even with shipping) mid-March, and this went pretty much to the top of the to-be-read stack.

While I've not read *all* of Godin's books (I believe this is the ninth I've gotten through), I've read a fairly representative chunk of them, and I feel pretty confident in saying that this one is something of an outlier in his work. Admittedly, this has roots in his Tribes[3], and has very much been echoed (albeit in a more "business plan" approach) in Chris Brogan's new The Freaks Shall Inherit the Earth[4], but this is more of a philosophical statement about "art" and owning one's art, however that is expressed.

Frankly, I wonder how this book would seem to folks who haven't read much of Godin. "Knowing where he's coming from" helps a lot to make sense of the more (on the surface) outlandish bits here ... as the thesis pushes the envelope on what is work, what is art, and how one can merge those into something that will produce an income in the new economy. As is so often the case in the Internet-connected world of billions of signals, *attention* is a key element (and often argued, the real currency of our age).

> *In a marketplace that's open to just about anyone, the only people we hear are the people we choose to hear. Media is cheap, sure, but attention is filtered, and it's virtually impossible to be heard unless the consumer gives us the ability to be heard. The more valuable someone's attention is, the harder it is to earn.*

In this Godin talks of "the connection economy", noting *"We're insatiable consumers of connection."*, and defines art and artists broadly:

> *An artist is someone who uses bravery, insight, creativity, and boldness to challenge the status quo. And an artist takes it (all of it, the work, the process, the feedback from those we seek to connect with) personally.*
>
> *Art isn't a result; it's a journey. The challenge of our time is to find a journey worthy of your heart and your soul.*

A concept he introduces here is the Japanese term *kamiwaza*, which is, roughly, "godlike" ... while this may seem hubristic to some, it plays to the notion of *creating*, which the artist must do ... he furthers this point with:

> *When we strip away the self-doubt and the artifice, when we embrace initiative and art, we are left with <u>kamiwaza</u>. The purity of doing it properly but without self-consciousness.*

This leads the reader back to the title character. Anybody familiar with the Greek myths recognizes Icarus as the son of the famed Daedalus, who had fabricated wings with wax holding them together in order to escape from King Minos. Godin argues that the part of the story which has been suppressed was that Icarus was not just instructed to not fly too close to the Sun (which melted the wax), but also not fly too low to the ocean. In other words, the Icarus myth is a "control mechanism" telling us not to attempt to achieve, and to accept the roles that society and industry have forged for us.

Two other concepts come in here, "the Lizard" (as in the "lizard brain"), and "the Resistance" ... the latter is all those escapes that come to mind to keep us from doing what we know we should be doing, and, in describing the former, Godin writes:

> *One part of us wants to climb the steps, to leap, to fly, to make an impact. The other, the more primitive one, wants to play it safe, to lie low, and to avoid failing.*
>
> *Our economy has worked overtime to emphasize and reward the lizard. We have built a society around making the artist the exception and heroism the rare instance that proves the rule.*

Which he later expands on:

> *Part of you ... is painfully aware of your potential. This part of your brain seeks respect, values achievement, and knows, truly knows, that you are capable of far more than you've done so far.*
>
> *The other part of your brain is afraid. The amygdala has evolved over millions of years to optimize its ability to turn you into a puddle of quivering jelly. This part of your brain has been amplified and given a free ride by the industrialists in power. We have been brain-washed by school, indoctrinated by industrial propaganda, and mesmerized by the popular media into believing that compliance is not only safe but right and necessary.*

Given that Godin is a business/marketing "guru" and theorist, the thrust of The Icarus Deception[5] is subversive to the point of being seditious. The underlying theme here is that we've been sold a bill of goods by those in power – in government, in business, and certainly in religion – and that there IS another way to be. The "connection economy" makes it possible, if not easy, to reach beyond those structures. How do we know how to find the way? Oddly, Godin says the irritations of The Resistance are key here:

> *The resistance is a symptom that you're on the right track. <u>The resistance is not something to be avoided; it's something to seek out.</u>*
>
> *That's the single most importance sentence in this book.*
>
> *The artist seeks out the feeling of the resistance and then tries to maximize it. ...*
>
> *... dare to turn your tabula rasa into something frightening, that's when you will begin to live the life of the artist. And the artist's constant companion is the screaming lizard brain.*

Again, this is not a "manual" for moving into post-industrialism, Godin writes: *"There are no step-by-step instructions or shortcuts in this book because those are easy to find elsewhere."*, however, he does provide a partial "Habits of Successful Artists" list to help one *"when the lizard is particularly wild, when the resistance will do anything at all to stop the work"*:

> *Learn to sell what you've made.*
> *Say thank you in writing.*
> *Speak in public.*
> *Fail often.*
> *See the world as it is.*
> *Make predictions.*
> *Teach others.*
> *Write daily.*
> *Connect others.*
> *Lead a tribe.*

He goes into examples that illustrate various aspect of being an artist, from Paula Poundstone to Christopher Columbus, with Dennis Kucinich and Don Quixote in between, and then ends with an appendix with "True-Life Stories of Fourteen Real Artists", but these aren't the Jackson Pollock *artists* (although earlier in the book Godin relates a fascinating story about Pollock and his teacher), but folks in the work world who have done extraordinary things, and in the process "made art". This is followed by a slightly whimsical appendix with an A-Z "Artist's Abecedary", which includes this:

> **Pain** *is the truth of art. Art is not a hobby or a pastime. It is the result of an internal battle royale, one between the quest for safety and the desire to matter.*

Needless to say, I found The Icarus Deception[6] quite inspiring ... so much so that I'm really hoping that I can convince my teenage daughters to read it, as they're in a position to take this to heart. It's available in hardcover, paperback, and e-book from the usual sources, and I think this is one of those "recommended to all and sundry", although if one is too connected to the "old world", you might find this unsettling. But I suspect Godin would suggest it's good to be unsettled!

Notes:

1. http://btripp-books.livejournal.com/155932.html
2. http://amzn.to/1CMW0oi
3. http://btripp-books.livejournal.com/104230.html
4. http://btripp-books.livejournal.com/155126.html
5-6. http://amzn.to/1CMW0oi

Saturday, May 24, 2014[1]

# Frankly, I prefer the Patti Smith version ...

OK ... this review is really taking me into new territory. For once I am VERY glad that I found the book at the dollar store, as I've since read horror stories about what ordering it via the late-night infomercials were like. It was, of course, due to having *seen* (OK, in passing while flipping through channels to see if anything worth watching was on at 3am) those infomercials that this jumped off the shelf at me.

As I've griped about on occasion, I'm in a long-time span of unemployment ... five years last week. So, the concept of being able to score some free-floating funds certainly appealed to me, and being able to snag a copy of this for a buck was great. You've no doubt heard that the author here has recently been sentenced to prison for 10 years, lucking out that his conviction was for "criminal contempt" rather than for fraud, which (his already having a couple of felonies racked up) could have ended up with 25 years of incarceration. With the awareness that this was one slippery character, I slogged into reading Kevin Trudeau's Free Money "They" Don't Want You to Know About[2]. As far as I know, he's not been brought to task for the contents of this book (unlike some of his *other* "They" titles), although I've read a few things on the web where people have complained that they were outright scammed by organizations *recommended* in here ... which is a bit unsettling.

One thing I'll give Trudeau: his style is light, engaging, and with just enough humor to take the edge off some of the more grim scenarios. If you didn't know any backstory on the guy, you'd like him ... I'm guessing that this is one of those books which was recorded to video and transcribed, as most of the expository parts sound very much like you're sitting around listening to him chat. There has also been some good amount of research involved here. Sure, most of the info could be found in a few hours on the web, but there's a lot of data in here, and numerous links for other info, be it news stories, or specific URLs for government sites that might not be so easy to dig up on one's own.

He repeatedly "baits the hook" with his insistence (and quotes from various sources backing him up) on how many *billions* of dollars get lost in the shuffle out there, and how many programs, both public and private, exist to distribute other *billions* of dollars. Trudeau is obviously no fan of the "They" groups in the world, and in this case he points fingers at the Congress, whose habit of stuffing bills full of obscure "pork" (which they then only inform their "in crowd" of), creates hard-to-find resources that are *intended* (despite the wording on the bills) to not be available to the "average Joe".

I actually *tried* one of the services he recommends early on, http://missingmoney.com, a service of a group called the "National Association of Unclaimed Property Administrators", which seems legit. I struck out completely with that search (nothing even *close* to me in their system), but it was pretty easy and straight forward ... and I anticipate that a good number of similar things are legit and usable in here. But some (as noted above) *aren't*, and the problem is sorting out the services from the scams.

Of course, that's supposedly what the book's about ... bringing together a lot of info from a lot of sources, saving you the trouble of digging it up on your own. I'm thinking that if one wasn't the brightest bulb in the box, and was uncomfortable with doing research, this book could be *very* appealing ... and he certainly sold a ton of them. There are 24 chapters here, most dealing with a particular area where one might find "free money" ... Savings Bonds, Bank Accounts, Tax Refunds/Credits/Etc., Pensions, Life Insurance, Veterans Benefits, Social Security, Class Action Suits, and more. In that part of the book, he does raise the reasonably plausible scenario that one's parents might have had some pension from an old job that didn't end up being updated, and that (and similar sorts of money) might still be out there. The next part of the book was about finding free stuff, medical care, legal help, and the like. One very odd thing in this is that he puts in *fourteen pages* of small print listings for legal services *in California* ... yes, it does give the impression of just how much stuff is out there, but serves very little purpose in the book, where it's useless to the rest of the country ... and the URL should have sufficed!

Also, my impression with these "legal services" were that the average middle class person fallen on hard times was unlikely to get much help there ... I was reminded of a time when an eastern European friend had been out of work in Chicago for a couple of years, and was trying to get some housing help for his family, and was told "that's not for you!" by the clerk in the appropriate government office, although he fit all the qualifications (coming from a socialist state, he was *enraged* at the "minority politics" in play here). Needless to say, my cynical side kept coming up, in reading these parts, with a lot of "like *that's* gonna happen!" moments – but that's in Chicago, you mileage may vary if you're in, say, Montana somewhere.

He then moves into looking at options about *housing*, ways to reduce your mortgage and loan payments, etc., and a lot of stuff about HUD and other groups that, again, sounded pretty Pollyanna-esque for my part of the world. But, again, there's enough solid info here (if approaching "common knowledge" on what one should be doing financially), that it doesn't read as something wasting the reader's time (let alone a scam).

Towards the end he addresses Grants and Foundations ... noting examples of some that are pretty narrow-focused (one offering grants for classical music grad students *"who need additional specific coaching lessons to make their professional debut"*), listing several dozen specific groups, and pointing the reader to resources (at the library) for more info. There's info on several government programs in there too ... such as a National Security program that provides graduate fellowships *"to study languages and cultures that are deemed important to to U.S. National security"* (I wonder how many of those markers got called in for the Urdu students over the past couple of decades).

Free Money[3] certainly isn't a magic tome that's going to unlock the treasure cave for most folks, but if one is "research impaired" it could be useful in getting pointed to place that *might* be helpful. On the other hand, Trudeau is a noted scamster[4], and there are stories of people being taken by groups that he recommends in the book. Admittedly, most of the complaints are from people ordering the book from the infomercials ... and since it's available elsewhere, that's a sucker bet. Now, the copy I found at the dollar store is the original 2009 version, and there's a new 2014 update out there ... which you *can* get through Amazon, but it evidently is just them selling through (at full cover) the book from Trudeau's organization (which would at least save you from inflated shipping and "mystery charges" to your credit card). It's available for a couple of bucks "like new" from the used vendors, but I can't really *recommend* this to anybody. It's not a bad read, but the info it has isn't some economic panacea, and there's the whole "scam" thing going on ... so only consider this at your own risk.

Or, as Patti Smith put it[5]:

> *Every night before I rest my head*
> *See those dollar bills go swirling 'round my bed.*
> *I know they're stolen, but I don't feel bad.*
> *I take that money, buy you things you never had.*

Notes:

1. http://btripp-books.livejournal.com/156331.html
2-3. http://amzn.to/1yHQXYB
4. http://www.consumeraffairs.com/health/trudeau.html
5. http://www.azlyrics.com/lyrics/pattismith/freemoney.html

Sunday, May 25, 2014[1]

# As platforms change ...

As those of you paying *way* too close attention to this space may recall, I won this and Likeable Business: Why Today's Consumers Demand More and How Leaders Can Deliver[2] a year or so back, for livetweeting the most from a talk Dave Kerpen was giving here. I might have gotten around to reading Likeable Social Media: How to Delight Your Customers, Create an Irresistible Brand, and Be Generally Amazing on Facebook (& Other Social Networks)[3] before now, but I'd lent it to some friends and only reasonably recently had it back in my to-be-read piles.

Now, this is a relatively current book, but I'm wondering with all the changes over at Facebook, if Kerpen is starting to regret his "hitching his wagon" to the whole "like" thing, given how devalued that's become. *Time* recently reported that in the most recent revision of how posts show up in members' FB newsfeeds dropped the average penetration to those who have "liked" your page from an already anemic 12% down to 6%, and I've seen other reports showing that trending even lower, to 3.5%, with rumors of things heading for a 1-2% reach. It wasn't too long ago that every company was clamoring to build up their Facebook pages, and get people to "like" them with the promise that what the brands posted would be at least potentially seen by the audience they'd built. I know I've had discussions about abandoning Facebook when pages that I'm involved with are only getting 2% of the eyeballs of people who have *expressed interest* (ie "liked") in seeing what's posted there. Frankly, in the time between reading the two books, the whole concept of "Like" has become a touchy subject for me, with it having a twisted "bait and switch" vibe to it now ... thanks, Zuckerberg.

I bring this up because it really IS a whole different world now than it was when Kerpen was writing this in 2011, and a lot of the specifics relating to Facebook are no doubt changed at this point, and a lot of the examples of how companies were reaching wide swaths of their customers are likewise no longer achievable under the new realities. How long are people going to expend the time and effort to make Facebook outreaches if only 2% of your audience is going to see it?

That being said, Likeable Social Media[4] is a fairly useful book on a "philosophical" basis, in the subtitle's "Delight Your Customers" area. Even if you throw out everything about Facebook, there's quality material here, from the Introduction's notes that:

> 1. Social media cannot make up for a bad product, company or organization.
> 2. Social Media won't lead to overnight sales success.
> 3. Social Media is not free.

... to the initial chapter's "Listen First, and Never Stop Listening", this starts with over-all good advice, even if the particular platform has gone over to the dark side. *"Listening is the single most important skill in social media, and one that's easy to forget once you get started with all of the sexier, more exciting things you can do."*

One note on a "structural" element that I really liked here ... each chapter ends up with a section of 3-4 "action items", and then a paragraph summing up the subject of that chapter. These provided a format that gave a sort of "manual" feel to this, with a plan for moving into the social media arena for those who hadn't been there yet.

Some of the advice in here relates to responding to comments, both good and bad (a chapter on each), with suggestions like:

> ... there's no way to entirely stop people from making negative posts about your company ... so, why not prepare yourself and, instead of avoiding it, embrace negative feedback, comments, and criticism?

This is in the context of "not deleting negative comments" (the first reaction of a lot of MBAs), leading into not ignoring them either. The author goes into ways of saying "I'm Sorry!" without your legal department busting bloodvessels over it sounding like admitting some actionable culpability ... *"If you can respond quickly and authentically, with an apology and a solution, you can avoid any damage to your reputation."*

One of the hardest lessons for a lot of MBAs, executives, and salespersons to "get" is the "Be Authentic" chapter ... *"Many large companies have a hard time being authentic in their interactions with customers."* ... attempting to maximize efficiencies with scripts, models, and processes, leading to the customer being subjected to the company's needs and not their own. Or, in the terms of a sub-header: "Authenticity Breeds Trust; Inauthenticity Breeds Fear". Similarly, there's the "Be Honest and Transparent" chapter, which highlights Kerpen's interaction with what he had been led to believe was a local State Senator ... only to find the Senator wasn't there, and that the entire social media outreach was designed to drive contributions ... followed by other examples of "astroturfing", where employees of companies posed as customers to come to the defense against legitimate hostile comments. This leads into a section about WOMMA (the Word of Mouth Marketing Association), and the guidelines it offers to keep one's interactions on the good side of the FTC.

Another chapter looks at how things improve if you *ask questions* of your social media audience ... not only can you find out what they're interested in within the context of your social channels, it can be like having a 24/7/365 focus group, with none of the expenses involved in running formal focus groups! This can even grow into actively "crowdsourcing" which can provide popular changes to existing products, line extensions (many companies have done this of late to get new flavors), etc. There is a chapter about providing free stuff (content) without expecting an immediate sales return, and another about sharing stories.

> When you hear the story of how a company was born, or one about the impact an organization has had on a customer's life ... you feel an emotional connection with that company. Social Media ... allow(s) you to share your stories with your customers, prospects, and the world, further building powerful connections.

And, once you've gotten the conversation started with *your* stories, you can reach out to get your customers to share *their* stories, since *"once people start seeing other customers posting their stories, it'll remind them of their own experiences that they might want to share."*, or:

> If you can connect with your customers on a deeper, more emotional level, you'll be much more likely to inspire them to share their stories about you with their friends, family and their own fans.

On the corporate side, Kerpen recommends that social media be infused into all areas that touch on the customer experience: advertising, marketing, PR, customer service, operations, sales, R&D, IT, and even senior management. A tall order, to be sure, but as he notes in another sub-heading: "Everyone and Everything Is Word-Of-Mouth Marketing".

Other chapters talk about owning up when your company screws up (and he has some very interesting case studies in this), and ideas to "consistently deliver excitement, surprise, and delight" ... leading up to a situation where you no longer have to *sell*, as your engaged audience of prospects will *buy* on their own accord.

Obviously, all of the above is "good advice" across all platforms, even if Likeable Social Media[5] is targeted primarily to Facebook ... the broad strokes (as above) are hardly specific to any one. There's lots of good stuff in this, even if it is focused on a old reality on a now less-useful Facebook. While this has been out a bit, it's still available in hardback, paperback, and e-book, with the online big boys having it at a fairly substantial discount (41% off at this writing). Oddly, the used channel is still right up around what the discounted new copies are going for, so it must be still pretty popular. Again, if you can filter out the Facebook specifics, there's still a very useful book here that is worth the read.

Notes:

1. http://btripp-books.livejournal.com/156574.html

2. http://btripp-books.livejournal.com/151272.html

3-5. http://amzn.to/1BBLumA

Saturday, June 21, 2014[1]

# So modern ...

As regular readers of this space know, I frequently take advantage of the *very* reasonably priced Dover Thrift Editions to nudge an on-line order across that magical free shipping line. As I've also previously noted, these provide an opportunity to plug holes in my otherwise-excellent Liberal Arts education – after all, you can't read *all* the classics in 4 years of college (especially if you're triple-majoring, but that's another story). So, that's how Henrik Ibsen's play, An Enemy of the People[2] recently found its way into my to-be-read pile.

Ibsen lived from 1828 to 1906, and had success relatively early in life, with his plays being published and staged as early as 1850, when he was 22, and had become artistic director of the Norwegian Theater in Oslo before he was 30. A series of reversals followed, however, and by 1864 he left Norway, not returning for nearly three decades.

I was impressed at how *modern* the themes of An Enemy of the People[3] are, despite coming from over a century ago (this was initially published in 1882). In it, a doctor (Dr. Thomas Stockmann) goes up against the establishment of his town, including his brother the Mayor, to try to stop work on a project he himself had previously proposed.

Dr. Stockmann is a significantly flawed character, very headstrong, highly opinionated, and certain that he's "the smartest person in the room" in every situation. He also has very little sense of how others process his pronouncements ... which leads him to being blind-sided by how events unfold.

O.K. ... since I'm usually reviewing *non-fiction* books, I am sort of "spoiler deaf", but I assume almost everything from this point on could be seen as "spoilers" to the plot ... you have been warned.

The key scenario of the play involves the town's new Baths, that have been developed to make the area a thriving tourist locale. The idea of the Baths had evidently been originated by Dr. Stockmann, and the facilities developed at considerable expense. However, corners had been cut, and the channel for the waters were originating at an easier-to-build source, rather than a more distant source as he had initially selected. In the time since the Baths had been open, there had been many mysterious illnesses coming to those who sought healing there ... from typhoid to various gastric conditions. Being the Medical Officer for the Baths, Dr. Stockmann began to, quietly, investigate this ... sending samples of the water off to be analyzed.

The play begins when these reports arrive, causing Dr. Stockmann to insist that the Baths be closed. He is under the delusion that his discovery of this will be widely hailed as saving the town, even instructing his early allies to not allow public spectacles being made about it. Ibsen writes Stockmann as a hard man to *like* as he, while generally *correct*, is quite insufferable in the way he expresses himself:

> The whole Bath establishment is a whited, poisoned sepulchre, I tell you – the gravest possible danger to the public health! All the nastiness up a Mölledal, all that stinking filth, is infecting the water in the conduit-pipes leading to the reservoir; and the same cursed, filthy poison oozes out on the shore too -
>
> ... {showing letter} Here it is! It proves the presence of decomposing organic matter in the water – it is full on infusoria. The water is absolutely dangerous to use, either internally or externally.

Despite this, the initial response comes as him saving the Baths following the "error" of the establishment of not getting the water from the more expensive source above tanneries at Mölledal, and finding allies in local householder organizations, and the town newspaper.

One of the more "modern" aspects here is that the newspaper staff is rather radical, and happy to have a go at the establishment. They essentially *goad* Dr. Stockmann into more and more incendiary rhetoric, and more heated encounters with his brother.

However, the "powers that be" in the town do *not* want to throw "good money after bad" to fix the problem, and do everything they can to suppress the information, and reframe the argument in terms of the Baths closing and the town losing not only all the forecasted revenue, but their investment as well. Bit by bit, the opinions are turned, and rather be the savior of the town (for bringing up the dangers of the current situation), Dr. Stockmann is made "the enemy", a dangerous person who is bent on destroying what they have.

Even his staunchest allies are turned ... the newspaper is faced with being shut out from the only available printing facilities, and a sea captain that has provided meeting space, etc., to air the health concerns over the Baths finds himself without a ship, pressure having been put on his employers. Dr. Stockmann's family is targeted: his daughter, the school teacher, is suddenly relieved of her positions, and his young sons sent home from school, because they had become a source of disturbance via constant attacks by the other students. Their house is subjected to stoning (breaking out most of the glass in the windows), and his wife's father-in-law (who owns one of the tanneries at Mölledal) writes her and the children out of his will.

Again, Dr. Stockmann is hardly a loveable character ... as all this is going on he only becomes more belligerent, and more extreme. Rather than being a doctor *serving* the community, or a crusader after its best interests, he turns on nearly everybody:

> *The majority <u>never</u> has right on its side. Never, I say! That is one of these social lies agains which an independent, intelligent man must wage war. Who is it that constitute the majority of the population in a country? Is it the clever folk or the stupid? I don't imagine that you will dispute the fact that at present the stupid people are in an absolutely overwhelming majority all the world over. But, good Lord! – you can never pretend that it is right that the stupid folk should govern the clever ones!*

The last part involves the phrase "does not dare do otherwise", in the face of public opinion. This comes up in an eviction notice, but is the spun out by Dr. Stockmann as the reaction of all those in conflict with the establishment. It is, perhaps, the last sane bit left to him, as he circles down to the point of declaring him the strongest man in town, if not the world, because *the strongest man in the world is he who stands most alone.*

An Enemy of the People[4] is a fascinating, fast (under 100 pages) read. If the above sounds interesting to you, consider picking it up. Your best bet is finding this on-line, as its meager $2.50 cover price makes it a hard economic proposition for the brick-and-mortar stores … and it might just save you shipping charges on one of those orders.

Notes:

1. http://btripp-books.livejournal.com/156769.html

2-4. http://amzn.to/1Eo5BTR

Sunday, June 22, 2014[1]

# Yo-ho-ho ...

This title may seem vaguely familiar to those of you who read this over in my personal blog, where I'd posted[2] a few weeks back a piece musing about how cool it would be if Disney and CBS would make a connection between *Pirates of the Caribbean*'s "Mr. Gibbs" and *NCIS*'s Leroy Jethro Gibbs. When poking around online, I'd discovered a book, The Pirates' Code Guidelines: A Booke for Those Who Desire to Keep to the Code and Live a Pirate's Life[3], credited to *PotC*'s Joshamee Gibbs ... and I thought that would be a great plot point to link the two characters. Of course, once I discovered that the book was out there, I had to snag a copy, and it worked its way into my reading pile as a bit of light diversion.

Obviously, this is a promotional effort for the *PotC* franchise, but it is also a fairly interesting read. I went a-Googling a bit to see how much this might have been based on information from National Geographic's traveling museum show, Real Pirates[4], which had come through Chicago (at the Field Museum) back in 2009. This came up due to some of the info in the book being nearly identical to my recall of parts of that exhibit. The exhibit began its US tour in 2007, which is the same year the book came out, so there might have been some borrowing there – or perhaps both were mining the same research sources!

I've looked at a couple of other books "based on" other media in the past, but I think this is the first time I've picked up something that I was reasonably well-versed on the source material (having seen all the PotC movies). I don't know if that's a plus or a minus here, however.

The pretense of the book is that the Black Pearl's First Mate, Joshamee (Mr.) Gibbs had, later in life, published a book about the Pirate's Code ... and that the paperback edition was a facsimile of that "long lost" book ... found, of all places, in a sealed chest in the wreckage of the *Titanic*. Not only was this a copy of the long-rumored book on the Code, but Gibbs' *own personal copy*, with amendments and additions (such as letters from associates such as Capt. Jack Sparrow, Will Turner, and Elizabeth Swann), notes scrawled in the margins, various bits and pieces of info taped in like a scrapbook, and even the change in the title from Code to Guidelines (as noted by Capt. Barbossa in one of the movies).

The book is full of art ... some of it basic and informative (illustrations of various knots, diagrams of the various sorts of sails, things showing how sails are places for running in relation to the wind, the various parts of a flintlock pistol, etc.) but the vast majority related to the movies, especially to *At World's End* which was coming out in 2007. Fans of the series will probably appreciate the art illustrating various characters (like the members of the Brethren Court), or specific elements of the films (such as Tia Dalma's fortune-telling crab claws), and illustrations of key scenes.

The text, likewise, varies between "scholarly" material related to pirates and their ships, and stuff that's purely from the story lines. There's a piece on sword fighting "by Will Turner", and instructions for playing "Liar's Dice", but most of the book is more concerned with how the ship was kept, how booty was divided, how they navigated, and quite a lot of detail on things like weaponry, sails, knots, etc.

As noted, The Pirates' ~~Code~~ Guidelines[5] reads like it could have been an accompanying volume for the Real Pirates exhibit, as much of the info is similar (if not identical) to what was presented in that. It helps, obviously, if one is familiar with the *Pirates of the Caribbean* films, as that would give the reader context for the *non-scholarly* bits. Overall, I felt that the Disney team that produced this did a very reasonable job of straddling the line between making a "real" pirates book and marketing ephemera for the movies. Your mileage, of course, may vary, since I've got both the films *and* the museum exhibit to refer to, and this might not seem quite so balanced (I could even see it being an irritation if one didn't know the movie side of the equation) to somebody not versed in either or both of those.

This has been out for a number of years, and appears to be out of print ... although a lot of copies are available via the used channels. I got my "like new" copy for 1¢ (plus $3.99 shipping), and there are still copies like that out there if this sounds like something you'd want to check out. Again, there is a lot of good-quality info in this for the history buffs, but it's also a nice "other look" at the *PotC* world. It might not be "for everybody", but could be a nice addition to a fan's library.

Notes:

1. http://btripp-books.livejournal.com/157036.html
2. http://btripp.livejournal.com/1186388.html
3. http://amzn.to/1Ja6qQT
4. http://events.nationalgeographic.com/events/exhibits/real-pirates/
5. http://amzn.to/1Ja6qQT

Saturday, July 12, 2014[1]

# Once upon a time ...

This is one of three books currently in my to-be-reviewed pile that got into my hands via the LibraryThing.com's "Early Reviewer" program. As I may have bitched about previously, the LTER "Almighty Algorithm" (which matches books to program participants) has seemingly deemed me to be a go-to guy for any business books that I might request ... despite the genre being a relatively recent feature in my library ... frequently coming in ahead of requested archaeology, religion, science, history, philosophy, and psychology titles – all of which are (I'm pretty sure) "deeper" in my collection. I bring this up (again) by way of providing some context: while I've read and reviewed quite a number of business/marketing/employment books over the past several years, they're in my reading more for their potential usefulness to me than any integral interest I might have for the subject.

I suspect that this makes me somewhat "less forgiving" for some books than somebody who spent a lifetime in the *study* of business ... and some of the reservations I have about Ed Catmull's Creativity, Inc.: Overcoming the Unseen Forces That Stand in the Way of True Inspiration[2] might not have been an issue for other readers.

Now, generally speaking, Creativity, Inc.[3] is a very engaging book, being a bit of an autobiography of Catmull himself, and a bit of a "bio" tracking the evolution of Pixar ... both of which are fascinating subjects. Catmull was one of the beneficiaries of "right place, right time, right skills" intersections back in the 1960's ... he'd early on wanted to be an animator (with Disney, of course), but was pretty sure his drawing skills weren't up to snuff for the big leagues, so went into the burgeoning computer field, just as it was beginning to drag itself out of the all-text swamps and discovering graphics. After working in industry as a programmer for a while, he returned to university in 1970, and got attached to a professor, Ivan Sutherland (who had developed one of the first computer graphics programs), who led him into making several major advancements in computer graphics, from texture mapping to spatial anti-aliasing. One of Catmull's projects was a 3D animation of his hand in 1972, which was featured in 1976's *Futureworld*, the first movie to use 3D computer graphics.

It gets harder and harder for the present-day reader to appreciate just how *recently* computers have become ubiquitous, and capable of the things we take for granted. Most folks in the mid-70's who were *able* to work with computers were hand-punching cards that were then bound in stacks, set into readers which would then punch a series of holes in a paper tape, which would then be fed into another machine at which point the data on the paper tape would get digitized onto magnetic tape that the computer could actually read and work with. For anybody who's done hand-coding ... imagine trying to debug that process ... where one might have, on a modern system, mistyped a comma for a semicolon (and have a color coded highlight showing you something wasn't right in the code), back in those days you'd have to go back to the boxes holding the stacks of 7.375x3.25" cards and try to figure out which card had the wrong hole punched in it. Obviously, Catmull and his associates were working on higher-end equipment by the mid-70's, but it was very much "feeling their way through" as all aspects of the graphics process (let alone animating anything) had to be invented as they went along.

Apple fans, of course, will find the presence of Steve Jobs in the story gripping. Catmull had been hired by LucasFilm in 1979 to develop digital elements for *Star Wars* and other projects, and he worked on the early versions of Pixar (when it was a high-end computer platform). Jobs bought the digital division from them in 1986 and over the years pumped in vast amounts of cash to keep it going – eventually they "pivoted", and concentrated on making movies, rather than the equipment. Catmull provides a perspective on Jobs which is not frequently presented ... including what it was like to "go to the mat" with him over points of contention.

Another long-time associate of Catmull, John Lasseter, had worked on an animated feature for Disney, *The Brave Little Toaster* (which featured digitally-produced backgrounds), and had been let go ... he was brought on to be the creative side of the equation at Pixar ... forming the core of the management team that re-defined the animation industry. Most of the book deals with the "behind the scenes" on making those movies happen. Especially in the early days, they'd be having to create systems to be able to get what they envisioned onto the screen ... but also there were cases where they'd determined that something was simply *not working* and completely re-writing the films.

O.K. ... now here come some of those caveats. There is a struggle in the book between the over-all historical/biographical sketch of Catmull's career and Pixar's development (which is the most attractivet part of the book), and sudden shifts in tone from "telling a good story" to ... well, almost being "school marm" in pontification on how elements from the story relate to "managing business in general". Obviously, at some point, Creativity, Inc.[4] was targeted to be a presentation on (in the words of the subtitle) *"Overcoming the Unseen Forces That Stand in the Way of True Inspiration"* ... and in reading it, I almost had the sense that there was an editor or project manager or somebody along those lines, calling him up to say "hey, we need more of that business stuff in there!". An example of this follows a tale about a road trip Catmull took at one point ... where he shifts from "telling the story" into:

> Now, consider this: The tire incident involved the interconnected models of just two people. In business, where dozens if not hundreds of people may work in close proximity, that effect multiplies quickly, and before you know it, these competing and often at-odds models lead to a kind of inertia that

> makes it difficult to change or respond well to challenges. The intertwining of many views is an unavoidable part of the culture, and unless you are careful, the conflicts that arise can keep groups of people locked into their restrictive viewpoints, even if, as is often the case, each member of the group is ordinarily open to better ideas.

Obviously, these sorts of "teaching moments" are worthwhile, and built on significantly keen experience, but when they come, they sufficiently change the tone to an extent that it *feels wrong*. If you don't mind me indulging in some "armchair editing", I think the book, as a whole, would have been far better served to have the *"now I'm going to impart the business lessons"* sections set off in boxes, and be free-standing *instruction* that then related back to the elements in the narrative from which they arose. Just sayin' ...

Anyway, Pixar developed some awesome movies, Jobs sells the company to Disney, there are "cultural" challenges (despite Catmull and Lasseter being thrilled to be there) to overcome, and lots of stories about films you've probably seen. There is also an afterword essentially memorializing Steve Jobs. The book has an arc through four sections that pretty much traces the Pixar story, and at various points there are the "teaching moments". Again, it's an entertaining read ... with lots of "insider stuff" on both the development of computer graphics and computer animation (and the movies based on it) ... but it reads like it's trying to be something more *pedagogical*, and that interferes with the story supporting those elements.

Creativity, Inc.[5] has just been out since April, so it's no doubt still easy to find in the brick-and-mortar book stores clinging to life out there ... and it's always a nice thing to support those guys ... but the on-line big boys have it currently at 40% off of cover ... making it quite reasonable to pick up. If you like Pixar's movies, or are interested in animation in general, or are a Steve Jobs fan, or want to know more about the evolution of computers as they developed into the graphic-intense beasties they are today, you'll certainly find something to grab your attention in this book.


Notes:

1. http://btripp-books.livejournal.com/157363.html
2-5. http://amzn.to/1KZ0yxD

Wednesday, July 23, 2014[1]

# For a particular audience ...

There is frequently a "pig in a poke" aspect to a lot of my book acquisitions these days, either being dollar store discoveries or review copies. In neither case is there a lot of consideration up front, but at least at the dollar store I'm able to thumb through the book. In the case of the LibraryThing.com "Early Reviewers" program, we get a paragraph of promo copy to decide if we're interested enough in the title to "request" it ... and frequently what's in the pitch isn't necessarily what's in the book.

This is one of those LTER books. J.V. Crum, III's Conscious Millionaire: Grow Your Business by Making a Difference[2] certainly *sounded* interesting – a guy who was following a newage/Buddhist path that turned his family business around into a multi-million dollar operation, and then sold it to go on to other projects ... and supposedly telling the reader how to do this too. Unfortunately, the book isn't so much a personal story as it is a pitch for his organization ... while the basic levels (which are *required* to actually "use" the book) are free, one gets the impression that he's going to be in your pocket sooner or later.

Now, I have a SERIOUS aversion to any of these "success seminar" kind of things, having been dragged through various permutations of that sort of circus over the years, and I have never run into one that was as profitable for the attendees as it was for the presenters. Just sayin'. So, when the author heads off in that direction in this book, he pretty much lost me. I was interested in a book about growing (or developing – the book is lagely targeted to folks already running companies) businesses "by making a difference", not an *indoctrination session* into whatever particular snake oil is waiting behind the curtain.

I also wanted to *read the book* not jump in and out of it to the ConsciousMillionaire.com site, but the book is structured to have you start all sorts of journals and workbooks. I was NOT interested in "taking his course" (at least not at first touch), and there was no practical way to get much out of this book unless you submit to those demands. And demands there are ... all through the book there are "Coaching" sections with stuff like this:

> Open your Conscious Millionaire Journal. Describe the value your business provides to each of the seven stakeholders. Also describe the value each stakeholder provides to your business.

I kept reacting *angrily* to these because A) I wasn't playing along with the Journal, B) I don't have a particular "business" to anchor this stuff on, and C) because of this, I'm not likely to have the *stakeholders* this section is talking about (which are 1 – Owner-Entrepreneur, 2 – Investors and Lenders, 3 – Team Members, 4 – Customers, 5 – Suppliers, 6 – Society and

Community, and 7 – Environment).

There was also a lot of material that didn't seem to make much sense in the course of the book ... he has an evolving pyramid with five levels: Conscious – Focus – Action – Result – Learning, with sub-divisions depending on the section (primarily in the "action" level) that kept appearing in each chapter, along with additional "Coaching" sections which, frankly, seemed like "wave a magic wand and have these swell things happen". There is a lot of saying stuff like: *"Select your top three to five business values. Communicate them to your team, customers, and suppliers."* ... but nothing concrete for any particular scenario.

I will admit that *maybe* if one had slavishly started the book with all the step-by-step journaling and worksheet assignments (and had a business with which to work), one might have something to extract one's specifics from ... but I did not "sign up" to take this guy's COURSE, just to read and review his BOOK.

There are some "nice" bits and pieces in Conscious Millionaire[3] which, if embraced by assorted business owners, would make them much less like the classic MBA cutthroats and more considerate for their community and world ... but, again, not much of this is concrete in the reading. It appears that the reason that this was in the LTER program was that it's a new paperback edition of a book whose hardcover was (in the words of a cover blurb) an "international bestseller".

If you are a business owner, and you want to *consciously* move towards being a millionaire, and are amenable to jumping into a whole system of self-assessments, you might get something of use out of this book. If you're hoping, however, to have an expository walk-through covering the subjects of the book, you're pretty much out of luck. The way this is structured, if you're not coming to it with a business that has "a team" and customers and suppliers that you have actual contact with, there's not much "there" there, as without delving into the stuff on the web site, it's pretty close to platitudes and wishful thinking.

Since this has only been out since March (oddly, the same date is on the Amazon page for the hardcover, so I have no idea how it got to be "an international bestseller"!), it's not gotten particularly cheap through any of the channels. However, unless you're in the niche for whom this is generally targeted, it's definitely one I'd suggest you skip – there's nothing in there of use to a reader, and especially one who is not already running a business.

Notes:

1. http://btripp-books.livejournal.com/157475.html
2-3. http://amzn.to/1xuu0IP

Friday, July 25, 2014[1]

# Sometimes things are worse than you imagined ...

I was somewhat surprised to have won this from the LibraryThing.com "Early Reviewer" program ... as I've kvetched about in here repeatedly, I seem to get picked for business books when I request them, and it's interesting to get something of a different genre. Since the month this was offered, I didn't request any business books, it showed up ... but I'm a bit unsure of how to define its specific genre. General Tony Zinni's (with Tony Koltz) Before the First Shots Are Fired: How America Can Win Or Lose Off The Battlefield[2] is a bit of a memoir, a bit of a military history book, and a bit of a political broadside. Frankly, it reminds me quite a bit of another LTER book I reviewed some time back, Kip Hawley's Permanent Emergency[3], a look at the TSA that gave serious "behind the scenes" access to the reader.

Zinni's Before the First Shots are Fired[4] is, at base, the author's stance on what went wrong in various military situations, and what he believes could be done about it. A product of the Viet Nam war (he joined the Marines *after* graduating from college in 1965), he was a participant in numerous military and quasi-military events over the next several decades. The book starts out with a look at historical data ... and it's amazing to think that in 1939 the total U.S. Military was 334,473 individuals (smaller than *Romania's*!) spread between the Army, Navy, and Marines (there were over 12 million by the end of WWII just six years later). Prior to WWII, we were generally not in a position to get in too much trouble (wars with Spain's colonies aside), but once the page turned from the end of that war and into the Cold War, we were all over the planet, and involved in everybody's business.

> *{The Cold War} left us with military commitments that our forefathers could never have imagined possible. We fought limited wars, counterinsurgencies, and "police actions" in Korea, Vietnam, and elsewhere. We supported armed struggles resisting communist takeover from Central America to Europe to Afghanistan to Southeast Asia. Clandestine operations helped overthrow communist or left-leaning governments in Iran and Central America.*
>
> *Unfortunately, these dirty little limited wars and military interventions turned out to be hard to manage. Our model was the "Good War" and we expected these new wars to play out according to that unambiguous model. They did not. They were messy, hard to define, and harder to sell, requiring tactics that in some cases seemed less than honorable – and not really true to American values. We supported dictators; we toppled governments; and we*

> *used clandestine methods to protect our interests and achieve our ends.*

One fascinating thing he notes is that every President had a military "doctrine" that was more-or-less formalized and served to guide military planning. What is somewhat creepy is that these, to a certain extent, never go away, so the strategic thrust of one administration is only modified by the next's (or subsequent), but never fully replaced.

Of course, as one would expect from a book by a General, much of this is pretty solidly from that side of the table, and the stories he tells of the *civilian* side are pretty horrifying. Every administration is different, naturally enough, and some came in with "the best minds" on hand to run things, but others were fraught with cronyism and worse (such as the Obama team assigning jobs more on the basis of campaign fundraising than any expertise, or even *familiarity*, with doled out cabinet or diplomatic assignments). There is always some cross-intent conflict between the sides, but it's amazing how bad this sort of thing can get when the politicians are trying to play politics with soldiers ... especially when the foreign excuse is largely a ploy for domestic results. I was, honestly, surprised with the rancor he reserved for G.W. Bush's administration ... as it appears that the key players in that (he particularly has a thing for Rumsfeld) pretty much didn't *care* what the military thought, and they were going to run things their way.

Zinni "lifts the curtain" on numerous conflicts and takes a look at the elements that were driving them, internationally, politically, and militarily. If you're a fan of military histories, these will be particularly of interest. However, the most fascinating thing here is how he frames "how we got here" ... from a fairly isolationist, largely rural, nation protected by oceans on either flank, to "the world's policeman", being pulled into nearly every conflict wherever on the globe it happens. He notes that the original form of the "Military-Industrial Complex" (a famous phrase from Eisenhower's "farewell address") was the "military-industrial-*congressional* complex", implicating Congress in a cycle that started with FDR's taking Depression-idled factories and turning them into the forges of "the arsenal of democracy" ... which soon enough turned into local "pork" that was unlikely to be ever taken off the books by Representatives looking at re-election every 2 years.

While he doesn't necessarily propose a solution for wresting control of foreign policy from the "military-industrial-congressional complex", while protecting it as much as possible from the craven politicization of it by the executive branch, he does discuss what he sees as positive programs, and what he sees as being deeply negative.

Before the First Shots are Fired[5] should be appealing to fans of military history, political intrigue, world history, and associated fields. While not being an auto-biography per se, it also traces out an arc of a rather fascinating military career. Unlike many of the LTER selections, this one is actually *early*, and the book won't be appearing until September, but you can pre-order it from the on-line big boys, currently at about a 25% discount. While I think this book could have been a stronger *statement* (Zinni obviously has tried to avoid "nailing his thesis to the doors" here), it's a fascinating look at a lot of the "sausage making" that goes on behind the gorier headlines, and I would certainly recommend it to anybody with interests in these areas.

Notes:

1. http://btripp-books.livejournal.com/157926.html
2. http://amzn.to/1yGNIGr
3. http://btripp-books.livejournal.com/150726.html
4-5. http://amzn.to/1yGNIGr

Sunday, July 27, 2014[1]

# Psi statistical analysis ...

I'm not sure at this juncture what had triggered my ordering this book, but it's been sitting in the to-be-read pile(s) for quite a while. I've read/reviewed another of Dean Radin's books previously (Entangled Minds[2]), and I seem to have been luke-warm towards that ... which is likewise the case here. I'm sure I'd seen his The Conscious Universe: The Scientific Truth of Psychic Phenomena[3] referenced elsewhere and it sounded interesting enough to snag off of Amazon ... however, I also took a read through some of the reviews there – which, while 85% run 4-5 stars, many also pointed out the book being "dry". Now, I don't particularly like to "prejudice" my reading of a book by delving too deeply into the reviews, but it did give me a context for the book, which was probably a good thing.

One of my complaints about the previous book was that he was constantly in a defensive posture towards the skeptics, and that same sort of stance is at play here, not as blatantly, but he's constantly pushing advanced statistical analysis of the data to the forefront, which, while certainly providing a "scientific" edge to the material discussed, *does* leave the narrative a bit on the arid side. This is too bad, as (much like in the other book) the studies he is looking at are both fascinating and provocative, and could have been presented with a bit more "gee whiz!" than creeps in here. I have to think that there is a middle ground between a totally woo-woo "AMAZING PSYCHIC POWERS!" sort of pop presentation, and this, which for much of it has all the sexiness of a report on comparative bridge load bearing data (that in-between niche is, perhaps, the realm of Rupert Sheldrake, in whose books I think I first encountered the sort of meta-analysis of study results that is the backbone of The Conscious Universe[4]).

Meta-analysis is where researchers take the results of many experiments and analyze them in relation to the whole. This could be done (as in one illustration in the book), with taking a baseball player's batting stats over a number of seasons to come up with an over-all stat for his capabilities at the plate (the movie *Money Ball* was anchored on a lot of this kind of number crunching). Here, examples of numerous sorts of Psi experiments are looked at together to produce "meta" results. If you would pardon a rather extensive quote, I found the following both indicative of the "tone" of the book, and revealing of the sort of rather remarkable numbers involved:

> Figure 5.3 shows the hit-rate point estimates and 95 percent confidence intervals of each of the twenty-five studies. As indicated, the overall hit rate for the combined 762 sessions was 37 percent. This hit rate corresponds to odds against chance of about a trillion to one – even though the majority of

> the individual studies (fourteen of twenty-five) were not independently "successful" (their 95 percent confidence intervals included chance). This again demonstrates the value of combining all available studies as opposed to just a few selected experiments.
>
> To show that the psi ganzfeld effect is larger than it first appears, let's compare it with the results of a widely publicized medical study investigating whether aspirin could prevent heart attacks ... That study was discontinued after six years because it had become abundantly clear that the aspirin treatment was effective, and it was considered unethical to keep the control group on placebo medication. This was widely publicized as a major medical breakthrough, but despite its practical importance, the <u>magnitude</u> of the aspirin effect is extremely small. Taking aspirin reduces the probability of a heart attack by a mere 0.8 percent compared with not taking aspirin (that's eight-tenths of one percentage point). This effect is about ten times smaller than the psi ganzfeld effect observed in the 1985 meta-analysis.

I'll admit that the specifics of the math still are a bit hazy (the 95% confidence intervals, for instance), but everything in the book is pretty much drawn through that knothole. Radin isn't quite "so defensive" in this volume, but he's certainly eager to point out where *other* fields are able to take *very* weak results and move forward with them as "proof positive" for an effect.

There is a certain defensiveness implicit here, however, as pointing out how tiny effects shown against a placebo or in response to some influence sets up a case where the *results* of the various psi experiments start looking "pretty impressive" in comparison. It's not like these experiments are regularly racking up 75-80% hit rates when "chance" would be 20-25% ... even the most hardened critics of psi would have a tough time maintaining their skepticism in the face of those sorts of numbers ... but this example, at 37%, is about as good as it gets – about half better than the chance result of 25%. While that's good and it's hard to dismiss (especially in light of the statistical voodoo which comes up with figures like that "trillion to one"), it's not particularly wowing to the uninvolved. Where a ballplayer will be in the Hall of Fame if he "fails" 2 out of 3 trials, getting only a bit more than 1/3rd right when pure random selection would yield 1-in-4 "hits" comes across more as somewhat "interesting" than really "convincing".

However, these are the results that are there, and Radin strives to make do with them as best he can. Ultimately, the argument *is* more convincing than not, with the statistical analysis churning through responses to most challenges. One thing that I found interesting was the "file-drawer effect", which is an argument that unsuccessful studies languish in files and don't get published (and added to the data in the meta-analysis). In most cases, the putative number of these unseen studies would have to be many times (often ridiculously so) more than all the published studies to be able reduce the effects of the analyzed data down to chance.

The Conscious Universe[5] is structured in four "thematic" sections – Motivation, Evidence, Understanding, and Implications – with "Evidence" being the bulk of the book. In this, the following are discussed and the data picked apart: Telepathy, Perception at a Distance, Perception Through Time, Mind-Matter Interaction, Mental Interactions with Living Organisms, Field Consciousness, Psi in the Casino, and Applications. The last two of these are fascinating in that there appear to be a ton of money being spent on Psi research within a handful of fields. Obviously, the Gaming industry wants to be able to manage any elements that could possibly effect its percentages, and there are some remarkably suggestive studies shown here (albeit with a rather small sample size as nearly all the big players were unwilling to discuss the subject with Radin). Other "applications" include the now-famous military studies, as well as ones done in the context of medicine and technology. There was even a 1982 experiment taking a non-investor psychic and having their stock picks go up against a group of 19 stock professionals … over the six-month study the psychic beat 18 of the 19's results, with an over-all gain of 17% for the psychic's stocks, vs. a 8% drop in the value of the stockbrokers! That's just one study with one psychic, but one wonders how many of the big investment houses might quietly have Psi divisions providing a different data stream than what shows up in the WSJ.

Again, if you're looking for a "rah-rah!" book for things in the Psi filed, this will no doubt be a disappointment to you, but if you're interested into delving deeply into an analysis of the data that's out there (and some of these data sets cover vast numbers of studies over long periods of time), it's a fascinating read. Sure, I would have like to have some more "preaching to the choir" myself, but you have to respect Radin for his reticence for flag waving, and staying with the statistical analysis as much as he does.

The Conscious Universe[6] came out in 1997, and the 2009 paperback edition is still in print, and must be reasonably popular as the new/used guys don't have either it or the hardcover at massive discounts. The on-line sources currently have it for about 30% off of cover, which is what I went with on this. I found it an interesting read, and if you don't mind the "academic" dryness of the presentation, you are likely to get a lot of very good info here.

Notes:

1. http://btripp-books.livejournal.com/158013.html
2. http://btripp-books.livejournal.com/86892.html
3-6. http://amzn.to/1C4LyKS

Monday, July 28, 2014[1]

# An oldie, but still a goodie ...

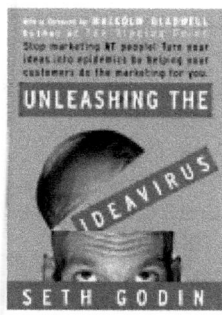

As regular readers of this space will recognize, I've read a *lot* of Seth Godin's stuff ... I'm about a dozen books in, but, frankly, that doesn't even qualify as *most*, as he's got 2-3 dozen books out at this point. Unleashing the Ideavirus: Stop Marketing AT People! Turn Your Ideas into Epidemics by Helping Your Customers Do the Marketing thing for You[2] is another one that's been around for quite a while, having initially come out in 2000, but it, oddly, does not have the "dated" feel that other books (his included) that hail from the dawn of the "social media/marketing" era have hanging over them. I'm guessing that this is because *Ideavirus* is more of a book on *theory* than one based on case studies (although it illustrates various points with concrete examples, and nearly half the page count is taken up by the "Case Studies and Riffs" section). Plus, his spiels on "permission marketing", etc. are pretty much evergreen in the current environment – which owes a lot to his vision of these trends.

Admittedly, Godin tries in this book to seed a new vocabulary for the spread of ideas, and this *may* be "patient zero" for the concept of message virality, but it's probably just as well that his terms like "sneezers" and "hives" (or "word of mouse" - which is *"word of mouth augmented by the power of online communication"*) didn't catch on ... although they are conceptually valid, and part of a complex of ideas that he defines as *"the eight underlying variables in the ideavirus formula"* (this latter is rather complex, and I'll spare you the details), which are: Sneezers, Hive, Velocity, Vector, Medium, Smoothness, Persistence, and Amplifier.

Obviously, he'd sought to come up with a *formula* for creating "viral" content, but if you've got eight variables in play it becomes pretty unwieldy fast (admittedly he does say *"No, I don't think you'll use it. But understanding the co-efficients makes it easier to see what's important and what's not."*), with a process that goes "multiply these five factors", "divide by the sum of these two factors", and "then multiply that by the product of these four factors" ... *sheesh!* He does go on to pick apart he "dynamics" of these elements, so while it's very complicated, it's not unclear.

Again, much of this cycles back to the "Permission Marketing" premise and *"the sad decline of interruption marketing"*:

> Unless you find a more cost-effective way to get your message out, your business is doomed. You can no longer survive by interrupting strangers with a message they don't want to hear, about a product they've never heard of, using methods that annoy them."

...although I suspect that he might have imagined that "interruption marketing" (standard advertising modalities) would have faded more in the decade and a half since he wrote this than they have.

That's brings me to one of the key dichotomies here, I think that history has shown that making something "go viral" is a lot more slippery proposition than Godin presents in Unleashing the Ideavirus[3]. Perhaps if one *was* able to effectively manipulate the 8 variables of his "ideavirus formula" (in their assorted permutations of mathematical massage), one might be able to posit creating at least a low-level "infection" on a regular basis, but we've seen so many companies (and individuals) throw a lot of time, money, effort, and intent at creating "viral" messages, that I suspect there's a lot more luck (and/or accidental superpositioning of campaigns with random elements in the cultural zeitgeist – which is a more plausible explanation for everything from "Pet Rocks" in the 70's to "Gangnam Style" more recently, than any marketing brilliance) involved.

On the other hand ... this is one of those *inspirational* reads, that makes the reader (assuming, I suppose, that the reader is of the "marketing" persuasion) want to gear up for a major project of getting Sneezers of various sorts to sneeze the viral message across the Hive, etc., etc., etc. And even the case studies (at this point being pretty close to "ancient history" in some cases) bring value, as they're here to illustrate dynamics of the whole Ideavirus concept, rather than as examples of things that might be copyable in today's economy.

At the end of the book Godin produces a list of "tactics" for generating "ideavirus" programs. He goes into more detail on each of these, but I thought the list was useful to give an idea of how he was envisioning this concept being put into action (on, I'm guessing, the agency level):

- *Make it virusworthy. {it needs to be "worth talking about"}*
- *Expose the idea. {even if you have to pay the target influencers/"sneezers"}*
- *Figure out what you want the sneezers to say. {controlling the message is important}*
- *Give the sneezers the tools they need to spread the virus. {make it easy to disperse}*
- *Once the consumer has volunteered his attention, get permission. {that's the name of the game, right?}*
- *Amaze your audience so that they will reinforce the virus and keep it growing. {nurture your attention}*
- *Admit that few viruses last forever. Embrace the lifecycle of the virus. {here again, I think the "zeitgeist" has a lot of influence of what works when}*

As noted, Unleashing the Ideavirus[4] has been out a long time, but it is still in print, and could very well have earned itself a slot on the shelves of your local brick-and-mortar book vendor. However, you can also get a "very good" used copy for as little as 1¢ (plus $3.99 shipping) via the on-line big boys' new/used vendors (which is where I got mine), if you're wanting to be frugal. I really enjoyed this one, and if you're into marketing, communications, social media, etc., you'll likely find good stuff in here as well.

Notes:

1. http://btripp-books.livejournal.com/158272.html
2-4. http://amzn.to/1uoBgEa

Saturday, August 9, 2014[1]

# Shaken, not stirred?

This is one of those books that I "got wind of" on the Internet, and shot a review copy request off to the publisher. I'd been familiar with Tech Cocktail for years, and have attended numerous of their events, and even exhibited (with the NLRWorms.com folks) at their recent Startup Showcase ... so, when I saw posts regarding their co-founder Frank Gruber's new Startup Mixology: Tech Cocktail's Guide to Building, Growing, and Celebrating Startup Success[2], I figured I'd reach out to the good folks at Wiley to get a copy.

There is no great mystery in what the book's about (it's pretty much spelled out in the sub-title – although one *might* wonder *"where are the drink recipes?"* from just looking at the book's spine), it's about startups, with a particular focus on the tech side of things. As almost my entire career has been in and around startups, this certainly had my attention from the get-go.

I've seen comments about this as being a "textbook" for the startup world, and while it *is* fairly inclusive of everything one needs to know or do (in the broad strokes, of course) to launch into an entrepreneurial effort, it's very much styled as a discussion ... with Gruber being in first person for much of the book, and outlining his experiences and those of a long list of fellow business starters (with both positive and negative results). While I'd agree that this would be a great book for everybody considering starting a business to read, I think it would be challenging to base *a course* on.

Startup Mixology[3] is structured in six "parts", which have two to four chapters each, these being broken up into specific topic sections, with side boxes featuring several dozen people, organizations, resources, etc., highlighting points in the various areas. I always feel like I'm being lazy when I do this (as you could get the info by flipping through the book or Amazon's "Look Inside" feature), but some books do well with a look at their "flow", so here's how this is set up:

> **Getting Started**
>> Entrepreneurial Mind
>> Ideas
>> Action
>> Formation
>
> **Product**
>> Product-Market Fit
>> Launch
>> Metrics
>
> **Team And People**
>> Team
>> Culture

>  Celebration
>  Relationships
> **Sales And Marketing**
>  Marketing
>  Sales
> **Money**
>  Bootstrapping
>  Funding
> **Growth And Change**
>  Failure
>  Success

Now, much of that list is pretty obvious, but other parts are less so ... some of the examples, for example, in "Product-Market Fit" are telling, and led to some fairly dramatic "pivots" from some great idea that nobody needed to something that is wanted: *"... if you don't listen to your customers ... you might spend a lot of time, money, and energy building an amazing piece of art that never sees the light of day or helps anyone"*. Another thing that might be surprising (especially to old-school types) is having "Celebration" deemed worthy of its own chapter. Needless to say, this isn't a "one size fits all" thing, and much of the chapter is given over to ways to determine what's right for one's own particular situation.

Zappos' Tony Hsieh casts a noticeable shadow across the book, from penning its Foreword, to being the subject of various stories and examples. Notable among these is, in the Culture chapter, where the "10 core values" of Zappos are listed ... oddly, this was only one of *two* things I bookmarked while reading through the book (again, the tone is more discursive than pedantic – leaving fewer "bits" to bring you here), but I'll spare you another list, especially as it's fairly specific to one business. However, Gruber does note: *"Company culture matters. Whether you're a startup or a large organization, the people who make up your business and the culture that guides it are critical to success."* ... and goes on to recommend Hsieh's book *Delivering Happiness*. Apparently Hsieh is also responsible for Tech Cocktail moving out to Las Vegas, as he leads "The Downtown Project", which is revitalization/investment effort to bring tech and related businesses to Sin City.

Having been in a number of startups, there are parts here which are both amusingly familiar, and poking at still-tender emotional scars. While almost all of the "Bootstrapping" chapter was painfully recognizable from my own career path, one thing that stood out in the Funding chapter was the concept of needing to build in a "fudge factor" in determining what sort of dollars you're looking for – as much as 50% over what your original estimates are – plus the aspect of "founder tuition", citing the example of one gal who estimated that she'd *"wasted half of her initial $1 million in angel funding on her own mistakes"*.

Obviously, this is not a Pollyanna-esque tract on the wonders of starting your own business. Much of the "philosophical" underpinnings are based on "lean startup methodology", and the "fail fast" school of thought, and there are cautionary tales throughout, and a "The Harsh Reality" section in each chapter (even in the "Success" chapter!). This does provide one with a *very* informed look at what hazards are out there, in a wide range of contexts and situations, and offers up examples of companies that have made it as well as those who didn't.

Again, the conversational approach that Gruber takes in Startup Mixology[4] makes this a quite accessible, if not necessarily "breezy", read – while providing a wealth of assembled wisdom from the individuals and companies discussed. This just came out at the end of June, so the business-oriented brick-and-mortar book vendors should certainly have it available, and the on-line big boys are currently offering it at about a quarter off of cover. If you have an interest in business in general, startup ventures in particular, or related fields, I think you'll get a lot out of this.

Notes:

1. http://btripp-books.livejournal.com/158668.html

2-4. http://amzn.to/1KXh2GD

Sunday, August 10, 2014[1]

# "It ain't what you want, it's what you need."

Here's another example of why I love picking up books at the dollar store ... the odds of my getting Jennifer 8. Lee's The Fortune Cookie Chronicles: Adventures in the World of Chinese Food[2] in any other context would be highly unlikely, but running into it amid the slim pickings (and *very* slim pickings for non-fiction) on the dollar store shelf made it a decided *"why not?"* add-in to my cart a couple of months back. Having spent the first decade plus of my career in food publicity, I do tend to have "food books" on my radar – but not to the extent that I particularly go looking for them – so I'm happy when an entertaining one comes my way.

Ms. Lee's book (and, yes, her middle name is the number 8 ... chosen to differentiate her from the other 10,000 "Jennifer Lee"s in the U.S., and reflecting Chinese numerology for good luck) is a delightful collection of "bits and pieces" (which appears to be the source meaning of "chop suey") related to the expansion of Chinese food globally, and how fortune cookies play into that.

The entry point for the narrative was a Powerball lottery draw back in 2005 ... when 110 people (vs. a statistical likelihood of a bit less than 4) all came up with second-place winning tickets, with nearly identical numbers (104 of the 110 played the same, non-winning, sixth number). The winners were from all over the country, so there was unlikely some sort of conspiracy to defraud the lottery ... but, naturally, an investigation was launched. From the lottery's perspective, having all those second-place winners was worse than having a bunch of first-place winners, since the big prize would have been split between the winners, while the second-place prizes were flat-rate six-figure pay-outs. By this point, you've no doubt guessed what turned out to have caused this mass of people playing a particular set of numbers – they had all decided to play numbers printed on the paper slips in fortune cookies, and that particular day the numbers in the cookies were substantially right.

Lee was a reporter with the *New York Times* who frequently got assigned to Chinese-American cultural stories, and she got sent out on an epic road trip – visiting all the restaurants where winners had identified getting the fortune cookies bearing the winning numbers ... visiting 42 states in all. One of the little factoids here that I found surprising is that there are more (primarily "mom & pop") Chinese restaurants in the U.S. than there are McDonald's, Burger King, and Kentucky Fried Chicken locations *combined* ... they are pretty much *everywhere*, woven through society, but in many ways only barely part *of* society. Lee traces the migration from various areas in China to the U.S. in different eras, both in relation to the titular pastry and in general.

Some folks might find it surprising that the fortune cookie is *not* a "Chinese" thing. While it could be argued to be an "American thing", the author's research eventually narrows down its origin to a particular Japanese "tea cake", which used to come with Japanese writing on its "fortune". This was brought over by Japanese immigrants in California, and had a small footprint of availability in Japanese settings there. The big change came with the Japanese internment in 1942. None of the Japanese-owned businesses continued in their original forms, with other Oriental groups taking over running them, or obtaining their resources. Among these were the machines for making the cookies, which suddenly were being produced with English copy, and being featured in Chinese restaurants.

Credit Lee with jumping the gap back to the pre-Internment Japanese origins of the fortune cookie, as there was a lot of confusion of who/what/when as far as the "originator" in the Chinese community, with various claimants, but very little hard evidence. While the fortune cookie question is the frame on which the book hangs, it is just one thread here. It also covers immigration, culture, the spread of recipes, and the function played by Chinese restaurants in the last century in the U.S.

Another "factoid" that I found of interest is that the reasonably ubiquitous delivery menu can be traced to a particular owner of a particular restaurant at a particular point in time. It amazes me that this model for getting food is as recent as it is (and, to be honest, I have a certain doubt about this being *the* start of delivery menus ... as I was able to call and have subs delivered to my dorm room in college at about the same time), but Lee points to one place on Manhattan's upper west side where the owner decided that *"If the customers didn't want to come to her, she would bring the food to them."* in November of 1976. The success that this one place was having soon exploded into nearly every Chinese (and other) restaurant adding phone ordered delivery to their business model. A related section later in the book discusses the dangers of being a food delivery person, with limited grasp of the language, in places like New York.

The look into the "underworld" of Chinese restaurants is fascinating ... from the cities in China where everybody has left to come to America (and sent home money to build big empty mansions), to the employment agencies and bus companies that exist to get (typically undocumented) workers to restaurant jobs around the country, to how these restaurants change hands (most move family-to-family as it is much easier than opening a new place with English-requiring forms and inspectors involved), and how various recipes evolved and moved across the country (and world). As noted above "chop suey" translates to "bits and pieces" and moved from California to the east coast, while General Tso's Chicken arose out east, and eventually moved on west (with many variations of the name ... Lee goes to China to find the original home of the General in question, and spins a number of stories off of that). Generally speaking, none of these "American" Chinese dishes have direct equivalents in actual Chinese cooking, and that the standard "American style" that we're familiar with here has become a cuisine of its own, with restaurants opening around the world offering those dishes.

A substantial side-story here was an idea that her editor at the *Times* came up with – determining "the best" Chinese restaurant in the world. Given the universality of "Chinese" restaurants around the planet, and the variability of style and influence, this was a huge challenge, but Lee visited candidates in Los Angeles, Lima, Paris, Singapore, London, Tokyo, Australia, San Francisco, Dubai, Seoul, Vancouver, Brazil, Mauritius, Mumbai, Jamaica, Rome, and New York, judging by a set of requirements to provide something of a baseline. The winner? A place located on the second floor of a suburban strip mall somewhere south of Vancouver, BC … go figure!

If I had a complaint about The Fortune Cookie Chronicles[3] it's that it heads off in so many directions, and becomes more of a collection of divergent pieces about Chinese "stuff" (loosely related to food) than something with a solid story arc. This is all *fascinating*, mind you (she gets into things like comparing Chinese restaurants to open-source software vs. the fast food icons being the Microsofts, etc. ... and where the "classic" fortunes come from – it's not Confucius), but by the end I was feeling like it could have hung together better than it ultimately does.

However, this is a minor quibble held up against the mass of incredibly interesting info that's in here. The book is very accessible, and pretty much "has something for everybody" in it. This has been out for a while (since 2008), and seems to still be in print in the paperback edition. Since it got into the dollar store channel, there are copies out there for a penny from the on-line new/used guys, including "like new" copies of the hardcover. This book was a great read for me (being a long-time fan of Chinese places), and if you're interested in any of the assorted sub-themes here, you'll probably like it as well.

Notes:

1. http://btripp-books.livejournal.com/158801.html
2-3. http://amzn.to/1wncvm2

Monday, August 25, 2014[1]

# Interesting, but very biased ...

As regular readers will appreciate, I've bitched a lot about the run of "business books" that I've ended up getting from the LibraryThing.com "Early Reviewer" program. It's not that I *mind* getting the genre (I do, after all, put in "requests" for those titles), but month after month it seemed like I'd always get the business book rather than any other sort of book that I might have indicated wanting.. As such, this month's book, Shortcut: How Analogies Reveal Connections, Spark Innovation, and Sell Our Greatest Ideas[2] by John Pollack was a bit of fresh air ... being a book more or less about *writing*.

I have a couple of qualms with this book, one being minor – the title – the body of the book does not really frame the subject of analogies in the context of being a "Shortcut" (although, one could obviously follow a twisty route to get to the point where one argued that an analogy was a "shortcut" from getting one's audience from mental point A to mental point B), and I sort of kept *waiting* for Pollack to get around to setting that up. I also had a "huh?" response to the cover, although I suppose the dominoes featured refer to the "domino theory" from the Vietnam war (mentioned in the book), with the middle one having the pips replaced with a winky emoticon – an analogy in and of itself, I suppose (although it didn't really work for me).

The second is a bit more personal, and philosophical, and can be expressed as a caveat: if your political stance is somewhere to the right of the smarmy Left-loving mass media, be prepared to be outright *insulted* at least a half dozen times through the book. Pollack was a speech writer for President Clinton, and his loyalties for the liberal end of the spectrum are very clear ... but in a way that is so off-the-cuff that one has to wonder if he's just another liberal who never exits the cesspool of Washington (or New York, or San Francisco) leftism, so assumes those muddy waters are just "the world as it is" ... much like the famous quote about Nixon's 1972 historic landslide election (over McGovern) by *New Yorker* writer Pauline Kael: "Nobody I know voted for him!". Repeatedly, he will shift from a very interesting, informative piece of exposition about how analogies work in various situations to a snarky hostile attack on some conservative figure. In only one case does he follow one of these muggings with a weak admission that "his side" is also guilty of similar "sins". I suspect that this is yet another example of the Left's regular version of "frat house sexism", assuming that everybody you're writing for has the same biases you do, and figuring you'll be scoring points by a "clever" attack that everybody can giggle about and agree what troglodytes those Republicans are. The fact that the tone shifts so dramatically in these attacks makes me assume that his editors "were in on the joke", since it would have *improved* the book to have excised them, and yet there they are.

These grievances having been aired, the rest of the book is interesting enough, drawing on literary, historical, and psychological sources to illustrate how analogies work in theory, and classic cases where they were key elements of famous speeches, etc. Pollack posits a model in which *"the most persuasive analogies achieve five things:*

1. *Use the familiar to explain something less familiar.*
2. *Highlight similarities and obscure differences.*
3. *Identify useful abstractions.*
4. *Tell a coherent story.*
5. *Resonate emotionally*

He takes these and "picks apart" several famous inventions and developments (as well as commercials and speeches) according to that model, including examples involving Copernicus, Gutenberg, Darwin, Ford's Edsel, Berners-Lee's "web", and exchanges between Bill Gates and Steve Jobs.

One element that I found fascinating is his relating the function of analogies to brain patterns revealed in the research of neuroscientist Benjamin Bergen of UCSD, which strongly reminded me of the Neuro-Linguistic Psychology materials I've read (although I don't believe Bergen's involved in that field).

> *"... {words} will trigger the firing of neurons that, to one degree or another, echo patterns created by ... actual experiences in our lives, or secondary knowledge of such experiences. According to Bergen's research and that of others, this is because we are using much of the same basic equipment in the brain to imagine {something} as we do when we actually see {that thing}. Similarly, if you are told to think about the actual motions you make in opening your front door, your brain will fire many of the same neurons as it does when you actually do open your door, except that in the imagined scenario, the brain inhibits the actual execution of those motions."*

Pollack takes this research to suggest an "analogical instinct" where the words shape the reality, and so are very influential in manipulating people's world views. To illustrate this, some famed speeches of history are examined, including Churchill's "Finest Hour" broadcasts, and Martin Luther King's "I Have a Dream" speech. Interestingly, both of these men were students of oratory, and the language structures involved. Churchill even published a paper[3] on the subject. Another example provided is how Franklin Roosevelt had to "sell" the American people on the idea of throwing in behind England at the start of WW2 ... using an analogy of lending one's neighbor a hose to help put out a fire in his house as a way to frame the huge expenditures that he was trying to get approved by Congress.

In the closing chapters the author bemoans how linguistic subtleties such as analogies have been progressively "dumbed down" out of the educational mainstream, including having the "analogies" section of the SAT exam removed by the College Board in 2005, replaced by an essay section. He quotes *New York Times* writer Adam Cohen on this:

> *"Intentionally misleading comparisons are becoming the dominant mode of public discourse ... the ability to tell true analogies from false ones has never been more important." While every American should be able to write well ... "... we would be better off with a nation of analogists."*

Shortcut[4] is one of the rare "Early Reviewer" titles which actually arrived "early", and it's still a couple of weeks from official publication. It will, no doubt, be out in the better-stocked brick-and-mortar locations mid-September, but the on-line big boys have it for pre-order, presently at about a 25% discount from cover price. Again, where this book fails is in its insensitivity to its (author's) biases, and how you will like it will no doubt depend on how deep you are into leftist groupthink. I suspect that most conservative readers would give it a "C" for interesting ideas and analysis, while your garden-variety liberal would gleefully give it an "A" for those factors, plus playing to their "in group" snickering. As noted above, a firmer hand on the editorial tiller could have fixed this problem by saying "no" to the partisan broadsides ... but "permissiveness" is a hallmark of that camp, so what can one expect.

Notes:

1. http://btripp-books.livejournal.com/159016.html

2. http://amzn.to/1J6bPs4

3. https://www.winstonchurchill.org/images/pdfs/for_educators/THE_SCAFFOLDING_OF_RHETORIC.pdf

4. http://amzn.to/1J6bPs4

Saturday, September 6, 2014[1]

# "Free" ... tasting of reality

I feel a need to apologize up front on this review ... I try, I really do, to get around to reviewing books when they're still fresh in my mind, but I think this is the third attempt I've made, going back at least a month, to get this reviewed (I noticed that it's right there in the to-be-reviewed pile sitting next to my netbook in a pic accompanying a Swarm check in[2] from August 8th) and my brain has "moved on", leaving me to pick through impressions and little slips of paper bookmarking bits here. Sorry about that.

Anyway, this was a delightful surprise to have found at the dollar store a while back ... I know I've discussed that channel *ad nauseam*, but I'm still thrilled to find something like Chris Anderson's Free: The Future of a Radical Price[3] at a price like that ($1 ... not quite "free", but close enough for my budget). If you don't know Anderson off the top of your head, he's the long-time Editor-in-Chief at *Wired* magazine, and the fellow who brought the world the highly influential concept of "the long tail" in his book by that name. In here, he is (obviously) looking at the trends to more and more free products and services, and how they fit into society in general, and how they can be sustained.

He starts by digging a bit into marketing history, first looking at Jell-O at the turn of the last century. In this case, to introduce a new sort of product, which was having no success getting into the groceries of the time, the company developed free cookbooks that its salesmen would go door-to-door giving away, and following up with the grocers suggesting that there was likely to be a demand manifesting in the near future for the product. In two years it went from negligible sales to a million dollars of product (huge for 1904) and in the next 25 years they distributed a quarter *billion* cookbooks in support of the packaged gelatin product. Next he considers the Gillette razor story ... in this case the blade maker didn't actually give away the razors – but they sold them to 3rd parties at such a low price that *they* (banks, etc.) could give them as freebies. And, of course, the razor without the blades was pretty useless, and men discovered that the disposable blades were a great convenience vs. keeping a traditional shaving blade sharp.

He also looks at the *psychology* of "free" ... one of the reasons that "micro-payment" systems have not been the success that one might suspect they could be is that ANY payment triggers a mental "red flag", referred to in the literature as *mental transaction costs* ... even if something is being charged as minimal a fee as a penny, it requires *"the mental energy of deciding if the whole thing is worth {it}"* ... so while these systems *"minimize the economic costs of choices, they still have all the cognitive costs"* ...

> So charging a price, any price, creates mental barrier that most people won't bother crossing. Free, in contrast, speeds right past that decision, increasing the number of people who will try something.

... or as NYU lecturer Clay Shirky notes: *"anyone offering content for free gains an advantage that can't be beaten, only matched"*. "Free" takes the whole "is it worth it" questions off the table, perhaps even at a subconscious level.

> Give a product away and it can go viral. Charge a single cent for it and you're in an entirely different business, one of clawing and scratching for every customer.

Anderson takes a spin through Moore's Law, and Mead's Law, and Alan Kay, who at Xerox's PARC in the 70's created the GUI that launched both the Macintosh and Windows (when first Apple and then IBM, respectively, stole the concept), on the concept that *"a technologist's job is not to figure out what technology is good for ... instead it is to make technology so cheap, easy to use, and ubiquitous that anybody can use it"*. Things were heading towards a state where they were "too cheap to matter".

He then looks at Microsoft (which managed to keep its OS *not* free), and Yahoo & Google's search and email tussles, and then peeks in at YouTube and the issue of "bandwidth" (once metered by ISPs – for the young'uns out there). He then circles back around to tangible vs. intangible product with a look at the encyclopedia market. In 1991 Britannica was the leader of a $1.2 billion dollar industry, with annual sales in the neighborhood of $650 million of $1,000+ per set encyclopedias. In 1993 Mircosoft introduced Encarta for $99 ... and by 1996 both the encyclopedia market as a whole, and Britannica's chunk of it had been halved (Microsoft had about $100 million of a $600 million category at that point). Of course, improvements in on-line connectivity and the arrival of Wikipedia put the final nails in that coffin, and by 2009 Microsoft had given up on Encarta ... with what had been a billion dollar plus industry reduced to a free web service.

The author introduces the economics term "network effects" to explain how this happens:

> In traditional markets, if there are three competitors, the number one company will get 60 percent share, number two will get 30 percent, and number three will get 5 percent. But in markets dominated by network effects, it can be closer to 95 percent, 5 percent, and 0 percent.

He follows with the example of how Craigslist, with its very modest beginnings, ended up gutting the newspaper industry, as the free listings and wide audience of the web vehicle easily became more appealing than paying the rates of the former cash-cow of print classified ads.

Free[4] eventually gets around to looking at the economics of these realities, from the theories of a 19th century economist, whose "Bertrand Competition" implies that *"In a competitive market, price falls to the marginal cost."*, this being a price just above the cost of production (which if you're talking something like MS Office, is the cost of a couple of CDs), to the reality that "every abundance creates a new scarcity", and in the world of nearly limitless information, "a wealth of information creates a poverty of attention". This leads into a look at Maslow's "pyramid of needs" and Adam Smith's "the science of choice under scarcity".

Towards the end of the book, it moves into a number of "lists", from a chapter where Anderson address a dozen or so "common complaints" about free models, to "Free Rules: The Ten Principles of Abundance Thinking" (the first of which is *"If it's digital, sooner or later it's going to be free."*), to a chapter on "Freemium Tactics", and "Fifty Business Models Built on Free".

Even though this has been out for five years, I never got the sense of this being "dated", as it looks at the whole "Free" question from a standpoint that's fairly evergreen, using examples that have largely played out to a point where they're not in flux, and basing most of its arguments on long-standing economic theory. I thought it was a fascinating read, and if you're into marketing, economics, web stuff, and related areas, I'm pretty sure you'll find a lot of useful info in this. This original hardcover edition appears to be out of print, but Amazon has two "bargain" editions – hardcover and paperback – which are *very* reasonably priced. The new/used vendors, however, do have it, as low as a penny for a "like new" copy, so if this sounds interesting, you don't have a big barrier to picking it up!

Notes:

1. http://btripp-books.livejournal.com/159356.html
2. http://bit.ly/1powTYa
3-4. http://amzn.to/1BwWrpz

Sunday, September 7, 2014[1]

# How the big boys are doing social ...

This is another book that I reached out to the publishers (in this case, the good folks at McGraw Hill) to get a review copy. Cheryl and Mark Burgess' The Social Employee: How Great Companies Make Social Media Work[2] sounded interesting, and I figured that it was something that would fit in with the general arc of my reviews.

To be honest, I was a bit worried in the early chapters here that I'd been "suckered into" something, as the Burgesses are the principals of Blue Focus Marketing®, and that "®" is, along with their "™'ed" model, all over the introductory material here, and I was thinking "oh, great, *another* long-form commercial for somebody's company". Fortunately, the pitch parts are largely limited to chapters 2 and 16, and the rest of the book not "branded".

Now, as regular readers of my reviews may recall, I have a system of using little bits of paper as bookmarks to get back to particularly interesting parts of a book – either for my own reference or for quotes for these reviews. While there isn't a "standard number" of these, I can recognize when there are more than average, and I found in excess of a dozen here (see pic ===>) ... so there was a lot of stuff that I found worthy of marking.

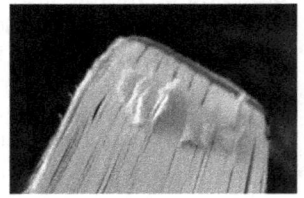

The book is in three sections, an introductory one which sets up the "social reality" and how it is, in the broad strokes, effecting businesses. The authors present their model for addressing "social employees", "social executives" and "social customers and prospects" in this, but don't beat the reader over the head with it ... and ultimately the take-away from this is that they're essentially defining their perspective, as a ground for what comes later in the book. There are several lists presented in various sections, and one here is particularly interesting: "The Six Most Irrational Concerns of Brands", which is something of a cheat sheet for pushing Social programs on hesitant upper management, as it answers many of the points that would be holding them back from being on-board with these. It is also in this section that they start to define what they mean by the "social employee":

> *Today's consumers expect online engagement with brands, and they expect to be engaged in an authentic manner. Consumers don't want to speak to a brand; they want to speak to real people. The rules of engagement for interpersonal interaction between social employees and customers are still largely unwritten. It is a certainty that employee voices matter, and that a brand's reputation de-*

*pends tremendously on how well its social employee representatives communicate with the outside world.*

This role is further defined by another list: "Seven Characteristics of the Social Employee" -

1. Engaged
2. Expects Integration of the Personal and Professional
3. Buys into the Brand's Story
4. Born Collaborator
5. Listens
6. Customer-Centric
7. Empowered Change Agent

The second section of the book, which is likely to be the "meat" of this for most readers, takes a remarkably detailed look at the social programs of a half dozen major corporations, IBM, Adobe, Dell, Cisco, Southwest, and AT&T (plus a couple of others that I'd not heard of). One thing I did note here, these are all (minus Southwest) tech companies, which might be logical in that they'd be presented with more organic opportunities to "go social" than companies in other niches. It would have been interesting, if just for variety's sake, if the authors had tracked down some other sorts of companies who were "doing it right" (I'm recalling Gary Vaynerchuk's Jab, Jab, Jab, Right Hook[3] as a source for numerous examples), but the focus here is very much on these tech big boys.

One of the fascinating aspects of this survey is how differently this group of organizations went about addressing the social marketing impetus within their ranks. I was particularly interested in reading how IBM approached this, as they still have a rather "starched shirt" image, and one would not suspect that they were particularly eager to cede control over company messages, yet:

> *Although expected to follow IBM's guidelines, employees' social activities are not centrally managed. This allows authentic dialogue to come about organically. According to IBM,* **over 400,000 employees** *engage the public, clients, and customers either through IBM-owned platforms ... or external platforms ...*

That's nearly a half a million voices ... with 26,000 individual blogs, 62,000 wikis, and communications traffic generating a whopping 50 million instant messages per day – all on their internal system. Add to this hundreds of thousands of Facebook, LinkedIn, and Twitter accounts, and that's a lot of company presence.

The section on Adobe is interesting in how they evolved over time. From a "centralized" model, they moved to "distributed", to "coordinated hub and spoke" to a "holistic" model. They've implemented what they call a "guard-rail" approach for corporate guidelines for social interaction by their employees. Another "look under the hood" availed the reader here is a fascinating chart that maps social KPIs to businesses objectives as a model of how they measure their social results.

The section on Dell deals with their Social Media and Communities (SMaC) group and their "university" social certification program. This program was envisioned to train 1,000 employees over a span of six months, but that had been exceeded within the first month – indicating the level of interest among the employee population.

In the Cisco chapter, there's an unusual focus on process … and this is charted out in a "WWHW Wheel" (What-Why-How-When) which tracks employee buy-in through awareness to understanding to belief to action and to outcome, with more than a dozen steps in between.

I wonder why AT&T is in the mix here, as they get a mere 4 pages discussing a blog program they'd implemented … given that all the other companies had much more material, it seems that this could have been edited out without lessening the book at all. Perhaps they're a current or potential client of the Burgesses and they didn't want to have them feel slighted by being left out.

The third section of The Social Employee[4] is something of a guide to implementation of what's gone before in the book. First looking at the "social executive" and what is involved in that role (including a list: "Seven Personalities of a Social Executive"), then on the need for educational support for training social workers, and look at various current platforms. The penultimate chapter deals with Content Marketing, giving examples of where this was done right, and another list, "Components of a Good Story":

1. Humanize
2. Be Distinctive
3. Keep It Simple
4. Be Viral-Ready
5. Transformation

Those last two largely encompass "shareability" and the concept that *"your content should leave the consumer in a different place than where they began"*. The book finishes up with their branded ("®"/"™") "10 Commandments of Brand Soul".

All in all, this book is a fascinating read in how it gets you inside these companies to see how they're managing large populations of employees. Unlike some other books aimed at company leaders, this doesn't have that "it won't do me any good because I don't run a big company" vibe - no doubt due to the "voyeuristic" aspects of getting to peek into the feature companies. The book has been out for a bit over a year at this point, so copies have worked their way into the used channel, but I'm guessing this can still be found in the business-oriented brick-and-mortar book vendors. Obviously, this one isn't for "all and sundry", but if you find social media on the corporate level attractive, it's definitely something you should consider getting.

Notes:

http://btripp-books.livejournal.com/159607.html

http://amzn.to/1BwVa1O

http://btripp-books.livejournal.com/151726.html

http://amzn.to/1BwVa1O

Thursday, October 9, 2014[1]

# On rosier planes ...

I've been trying to get caught up with my Library Thing "Early Reviewer" reading ... back when I was plowing through six books a month, having that month's LTER "win" in the mix wasn't much of a problem, but these days when I'm lucky to get *three* books done in a month, I'm having to make sure I muscle those into the queue.

Needless to say, Jim Davies' Riveted: The Science of Why Jokes Make Us Laugh, Movies Make Us Cry, and Religion Makes Us Feel One with the Universe[2] was a LTER selection (or I'd not be mentioning it, would I?), and a fairly recent one at that. As you no doubt recall, I'd been getting bitchy about all the "business books" that I'd had from that channel over the past year of so, so I was pretty happy to have a science book show up!

Given this, I really had hoped to have *liked* Davies' book more than I did. I'm pretty sure that this is one of those "your mileage may vary" instances, but for me, at least, I came away with a sense that it meandered (indeed, at one point the author describes it as *"super lumpy"*), didn't solidly *build* point-to-point, and was given to making pronouncements that were not particularly convincing on their surface (for instance, while he, rather credibly, assigns an evolutionary role of the avoidance of rubber snakes by birds in places that have *no snakes* - suggesting that some ancient predecessor of said birds had developed a hard-wired reaction to the shape that carried down to the present ... he also asserts that the Northern European's ability to digest milk past infancy was a *culturally* derived trait based on "a desire to drink milk" which drove the genetic shift – this appearing notably *without* a source attribution).

I don't typically read other people's reviews before digging into a book, but my curiosity was piqued by the relatively low star rating that this had over on LibraryThing. Others there had some similar issues as I ended up with in terms of focus, etc., but there was also a sub-theme of the broadsides that Davies launches at religion. Now, as regular readers of this space know, I'm a deep agnostic when it comes to organized religions, but am also given to a rather promiscuous openness when it comes to metaphysical/spiritual topics. Where I was the choir being preached to in sections like:

> *If you hear something {health related} that you hope or fear is true, treat it with skepticism, because there are forces within you suppressing your doubts.*
>
> \* \* \*
>
> *Like medical quackery, religion too is filled with hope and fear. Christianity, Hinduism, and Islam, in particular, have a great deal to say about what risk*

> one takes by not following their edicts and the benefits to be experienced in following them, both now and in an afterlife.

I also found myself mentally countering him (a bit like Graham Hancock critiquing Richard Dawkins) when it came to rather blanket insistence that *all* spiritual experience originated in electric or chemical processes in the brain.

The book is in seven sections, each taking on a different area for looking at our interfaces with the world. These are, generally: socialization, hope & fear, pattern perception, incongruity and the like, biological nature, psychological biases, and the foundations of compellingness. Each is full of references to various types of studies (and in a full spectrum of style: from offhand nods to a particular theory to back-noted details of the research), with the author "patting himself on the back" for his thoroughness: *"It's easy to cherry pick evidence to support these ideas, so I took care to report any counterevidence I discovered."*. Frankly, I might have preferred this had Davies taken each of those sections and fleshed it out into a small book *on that one aspect* and released the seven as a boxed set. That would have (hopefully) provided him with the "breathing room" to make a coherent statement about each area, which could (perhaps with an eighth book to pull "the broad strokes" of the others together) have been a far more convincing statement than Riveted[3] ends up being.

Again, while these *structural* complaints are not trivial, they don't necessarily diminish the value of the book. There is an awful lot of very interesting *stuff* in here, just in a form that is less accessible and persuasive that it might have been. Of the sections of the book, I probably found the "incongruity" section (the "Incongruity: Absurdism, Mystery, and Puzzle" chapter) the most fascinating, and am somewhat frustrated that the individual points brought up in there (which could have been built into workable chapters in an "Incongruity" book) sort of flash by with just enough detail draw one in, before moving on to the next thing. In this he discusses physical evolutionary pressures (newborn brain size vs. the size of the birth canal), art, movies, sports, and music (including the concept of "categorical perception" which leads to mental "autocorrection" in *experts* but not in people untrained in music – the pro will hear a slightly-off note as the *intended* note, while the novice will be more sensitive to the actual pitch), product design (people prefer "conventional" design, but with one unusual feature), and many more. Incongruity is contrasted with pattern recognition, and between them the fact that we start by preferring the familiar, but become bored, and move towards the unusual … this is why it's more exciting to root for a sports team that wins by small margins and dramatic finishes, than one that steamrolls it's competition game after game.

There is also an on-going theme of "old brain" vs. "new brain", which plays into everything from tribalism to religion and beyond. In the introduction Davies presents a very concrete example (in this case, encountering a pack of cupcakes), the dynamics of which everybody should find familiar:

> *The old brain "knows" that sugar and fat are scarce and should always be eaten when the opportunity arises. Thousands of years of evolution taught it that. It doesn't know that fat, sugar, and salt are now plentiful and contributing to an obesity problem in the industrial world. In contrast, the new brain knows that too much sugar isn't good for you. But who are you going to listen to?*

That last bit is indicative of the humor that's woven through the various parts of the book. One *could* argue that this lends a somewhat flippant attitude to the text, but I didn't find it objectionable.

While Riveted[4] was not as wonderful read as I'd hoped it would be, it certainly provided a whole lot of "food for thought". As noted, I did find it rambling and uneven, but in a way that had me wanting *more* rather than less. This just came out in August, so should certainly be out in those remaining brick-and-mortar book stores that handle science. Of course, the online big boys have it, with the current offering being at about ten bucks off of the cover price.

Notes:

1. http://btripp-books.livejournal.com/159822.html

2-4. http://amzn.to/1xrPL5O

Saturday, October 11, 2014[1]

# A difficult subject ...

Here's another book that came my way via LibraryThing.com and their "Early Reviewer" program ... a member benefit on LT where publishers make a certain number of books available each month, and LT users can request copies. I've been in the program from the start, and have only missed getting a book assigned to me by "The Almighty Algorithm" a handful of times (usually when I just requested ONE book) over the past 3-4 years.

Needless to say, Sylvia Longmire's Border Insecurity: Why Big Money, Fences, and Drones Aren't Making Us Safer[2] is remarkably topical ... and reasonably up-to-date, having come out just a few months back (of course, the way things go with "current events" sorts of books, that's well before the current Ebola scare, so that level of border concern is only peripherally addressed here).

Ms. Longmire's bio reads like something out of the NCIS television franchise ... except that she's a former Air Force Captain and Special Agent in the Air Force Office of Special Investigations, who operated in numerous governmental agencies as an intelligence analyst since her medical retirement (for the effects of MS), and has recently been principal of Longmire Consulting ... with special expertise on the Southern border, both via her many assignments dealing with Latin American intel, her Cuban-American background, and the research involved in developing her previous book, *Cartel*. Needless to say, she's neither an armchair security dilettante nor a kumbayah-singing hand-wringer on the subject of immigration.

Border Insecurity[3] is certainly an "eye-opener" ... there was all sorts of stuff that I had *no idea* about. First of all, much of the border is only sort of defined ... with "defenses" that might make it difficult to drive a pickup truck through, but being only a minor inconvenience for those coming through on foot (and there being regular gaps where semitrailers could make it through). Sure, there are very visible portions of the border with serious walls, and all sorts of surveillance equipment, but these tend to only show up in the area of larger border towns, and soon peter out to rebar and chainlink.

The other element here is the naked brutality of the drug cartels. Much like non-commercial terrorist organizations, most of these groups are vicious, callous, and more than willing to commit atrocities just to make a point. The stories that are in here of these sorts of things (whole villages being rounded up, massacred, and their bodies put on display) are shocking. The cartels force numerous groups (even some from other parts of Latin America, trying to reach the US), to carry drugs across the borders, and if there is anything other than total cooperation, they're killed. And, if they're sent *back* across the border, they're killed ... often by Mexican police working for the drug lords. One quote that Longmire offers up here is *"Immigration judges are doing death penalty cases in traffic court settings."*

Recently, rules established to handle the cases of people from *"places like Haiti, Guatemala, Romania, and Iraq"* who have a "credible fear" leading to them requesting asylum, have been leveraged by Mexicans, and the rules for claiming this (understandably, in the context of the drug gangs' brutality) have totally back-logged the system:

> *Any time that an immigrant does this, whether it's at a port of entry with a CBP agent or in the middle of the Arizona desert with a Border Patrol agent, everything has to come to a halt. By law, CBP and Border Patrol have to conduct a "credible fear" interview of the immigrant, meaning that they have to determine exactly why they're afraid to return to their home country. This process also ensures that, if the immigrant's story meets the credible fear threshold, he or she will have his or her day in court before an immigration judge.*

Of course, there's no system for keeping masses of asylum-seekers while they wait for their court date and, according to the Immigration and Customs Enforcement organization, *"between 600,000 and 800,000 illegal immigrants fail to show up for their hearings every year"*.

One of the more disturbing bits here is how Islamic terrorists are shipping their agents to places in Latin America, where they're given a chance to learn enough Spanish and cultural patterns, and then come across with other illegals. There's 2,000 miles of border between the US and Mexico, and well less than half of that has even been addressed with modern systems.

Speaking of "modern systems", it is horrifying how much money has been poured into border initiatives with so little effect. Much like anything the government does, as soon as a budget is approved, there are hundreds, if not thousands, of quick-buck seekers lining up at the trough. Too often these groups have figured out a minimum compliance to the specifications of the new program, and cobble together enough off-the-shelf materials to *look* to government examiners that they're just a few hundred grand away from going into full production. There are numerous examples of these sorts of "ghost deals" where the money was spent for inefficient or purely illusory "solutions".

Of course, the 800lb gorilla here is that the Mexican government is often complicit in both the drug and the terror trade ... or, if not *complicit*, at least "looking the other way" when convenient to the cartels and Islamists. Obviously, this is NOT a subject that certain portions of *our* government wants to admit exists ... although there are some waking up to it. Longmire notes in her conclusion:

> *Out of terrorists, drug traffickers, and illegal immigrants, the last group is the only one that poses no threat to our national security, and coincidentally is*

> the easiest one to manage through legislation alone. Finding a way to convert illegal immigration from an enforcement issue to a policy issue is critical to improving border security across the United States. ... Imagine a situation where migrants wishing to work in the United States could go through a standardized and streamlined process of applying for a guest worker visa (or similar temporary program) and go through all the background checks in their home countries. Or a situation where millions of immigrants who overstayed their visas and have been living here illegally for years can affirmatively apply for cancellation of removal and start paying taxes. ... with significantly reduced numbers of economic migrants crossing our borders, DHS could prioritize threats and refocus its limited resources toward detecting and apprehending violent criminals and terrorists.

There is also a chapter in here addressing the issues of the *Canadian* border, but that's evidently not the author's area of expertise, and, to a large extent is a different situation in several key factors. At present it appears that the threat of Islamic terrorists getting into the US is more substantial via the Northern border, as there are significant enclaves of various Muslim groups throughout Canada's major cities. Also, there is a drug trade, involving biker gangs and Asian cartels, but nothing near the volume or viciousness of the Mexican border.

Border Insecurity[4] is a fascinating, very scary, and quite frustrating read which puts a lot of things into context, but really doesn't (can't?) offer up a lot of solutions aside from the idea that "economic migration" needs to be decoupled from the "drugs & terror" elements, and dealt with in a way that's advantageous to both the US economy and the aspirations of the migrants. Although this has only been out a half a year, much of the "news" has raced past what's in this, but it provides a solid look at aspects of a major problem, throwing light on aspects which most folks haven't encountered.

Notes:

1. http://btripp-books.livejournal.com/160200.html
2-4. http://amzn.to/1EjvNyR

Tuesday, October 21, 2014[1]

# Connecting with the customer ...

I was very excited to get Scott Stratten's new book, Un-Selling: The New Customer Experience[2], having requested a review copy from the good folks at Wiley as soon as I'd seen Scott talking about it online. As regular readers recall, I've read all of his previous releases, and UnMarketing[3] has been one of my go-to books to familiarize folks (who have been living in caves) with the general concepts of Social Media.

I may have been oblivious, but this is the first book that I've noticed has credited Alison Kramer as a co-author on the cover ... the Amazon listings of Scott's other books (and the revised edition of UnMarketing) list her as a co-author, but poking through the "Look Inside" view, she's neither on the cover, the title page, or in the copyright ... which I find slightly odd. I know that Scott's been crediting her with involvement during their podcasts, etc., but as far as I can tell this is the first time she's "in ink" (although still not credited in the copyright ... but that might be "a Canadian thing").

This book is an easy read, being split up into 60 chapters, each only being a few pages long, making each topic "bite size", and perfect for consumption on public transportation! Most are based on "stories" of Social Media ... or "Customer Experience" (as per the subtitle) ... being done well or (more frequently not) by various companies and organizations. One thing that is notably different in UnSelling[4] is that there's a "model" being floated. Scott's books have generally been off in a grey zone between "philosophy" of Social, and rants-in-print about clueless practitioners. However, it appears to be de rigueur for any guru putting out a marketing book to come up with their own "system" about how things work, and I guess that Scott (and Alison?) decided that they were falling behind not having one of their own.

Hence the "UnSelling" model. Now, I want to point out that the authors *don't* beat the reader over the head with this concept, but they do return to it every now and again, so it's important to "get" in the context of the book. Here are a couple of bits where this starts to get framed:

> UnSelling is what happens when you understand the humanity of your market, produce a quality product, and create experiences that lead to trusted referrals. UnSelling means stepping back from the funnel and focusing on everything else but the sale. ...
>
> In UnSelling you will see how your experiences as a consumer matter and shape your choices and the choices of those around you, and you will see that your experiences as a business matter and can

> *change industries and create growth. In <u>UnSelling</u>, good experience is good business.*

To preface the *UnSelling* model, first marketers need to breakout of "Funnel Vision" ... the traditional concept of the "sales funnel" (and assorted new permutations of this). Stratten cites figures that *"60 percent of all purchase decisions are made before customers enter your funnel"*, and points to Sprout Social's research that *"74 percent of customers {rely} on social networks to guide purchase decisions"*, with consumers checking with as many as *"20 resources before making a click through to purchase decision"*.

The key concept in the *UnSelling* model is called "Pulse", and it's represented as a graph like what would be traced out by a heart monitor. The background is divided into three bands: Vulnerable – *"where people are most open to competition"*, Static – this is the main zone in which the customer and the brand interact, and Ecstatic – where you find *"brand fans and ambassadors"* (*"Static customers exist, but ecstatic customers refer. We should be doing everything we can, every single day in business to move individuals into this space."*). The graph is further defined:

> Each point of contact between the brand and individual is called a <u>pulse point</u>. This is where we can measure the relationship between the brand and its market at any time. Because there is no such thing as a neutral brand experience, the line is always moving.

Except that it can also stop moving ... or *flatline*, this is when brand experience has become sufficiently bad that the consumer walks away from it.

> When the bottom falls out on pulse, we see a <u>flatline</u>. This is the definitive end of the relationship and an opportunity for competitors. The flatline is very important in social media because it is extreme. Extreme experiences, both good and bad, are always shared the most online. When a flatline happens, people will take to social media ... to share their horror stories.

The pulse points are determined by two sets of influences, *external factors*, forces from the brand (not within control of the individual), and *internal factors*, which are the customer's purchase decisions and reactions to the brand, and these are broken down into "AIM" – Aspiration, Information, and Motivation.

While I was being a bit snarky up above when I noted they return to this model "every now and again", I don't think I'm being unrealistic. Once the UnSelling/Pulse model is sketched out, the book largely shifts to Scott telling his stories ... which are, of course, delightful and/or horrific. Now, I've been an "UnMarketing consumer" for quite a while and have heard Scott talk in person, on video, and via podcast, as well as reading his blog posts, tweets, and Facebook entries (not to mention having read and reviewed his three previous books), so I've had a lot of opportunity to have been exposed to his favorite examples, and I have to admit that a lot of the "case studies" here are at least somewhat familiar. From the heart-warming story of how the Ritz-Carlton rescued a young lad's favorite stuffed animal (and created a whole "vacation story" of what said critter had been up to in its absence), to the equally heart-warming story of a developmentally disabled kid whose whole childhood (really, it could have been that bad) was saved by some Disney staffers making an extra effort to make sure he had the Star Wars experience that he'd fixated on, to Scott's journey through Hell with Delta (or the rage-induced "Detla"), which through some fast response turned him into a fan ... I've heard them before. Of course, these are "big finish" stories that I'm sure he tells regularly from the convention dais, but a sense of *"what else ya got?"* is likely to creep in a bit among his fans. This is not to say that there isn't a *wealth* of horror stories that made the "UnAwesome" side of *Awsome/UnAwesome* such a festival of *schadenfreude*, and fun examples of organizations using social in delightful ways (like the York Regional Police responding to a Twitter-scheduled drug deal with *"Awesome! Can we come too?"*) ... but you do sort of feel the struggle to balance re-using "core material" with moving forward with new stuff.

Towards the latter part of the book, another concept, the "pivotpoint" (where the pulse line changes directions dramatically) is thrown into the UnSelling model mix, with examples of *"successful companies {that} were not afraid to make big changes when presented with industry and technology shifts"* ... with Scott amusingly comparing what these various organizations and company founders did, versus his response to similar triggers.

Again, UnSelling[5] is an entertaining and informative book, but could have been better with a bit more focus. As interesting as the "Pulse" model is, the book wasn't structured to support it, rather being much more about "The New Customer Experience", with the Pulse stuff being a particular frame for that, but hardly being the definitive element (i.e. had this been a book titled *Pulse: Achieving the Ecstatic, Avoiding the Vulnerable*). Of course, maybe that's Scott. Maybe he doesn't have the hubris needed to issue an "I Am A Marketing Guru And This Is My System" book that would take itself seriously cover-to-cover. That's not a bad thing, but in this case the two poles of the book never seemed to develop a central stable theme. UnSelling[6] came out just a few weeks ago, so it should be out there in the brick-and-mortar booksellers, and the on-line big boys have it, of course, at about a quarter off of cover price. Generally speaking, I really liked it, but then again I'm a Stratten/Kramer fanboi ... still, if you have any interest in marketing, social media, and related niches, you should get quite a bit from picking this up.

Notes:
1. http://btripp-books.livejournal.com/160423.html
2. http://amzn.to/1u9PTLF
3. http://btripp-books.livejournal.com/101421.html
4-6. http://amzn.to/1u9PTLF

Wednesday, October 22, 2014[1]

# The problem with "used" ...

OK ... I feel bad about this. Really. Some time ago I had put Shama Hyder Kabani's The Zen of Social Media Marketing: An Easier Way to Build Credibility, Generate Buzz, and Increase Revenue[2] on my Amazon "wish list", which is generally where I park books that I want, but not necessarily "right now". I suspect that part of what drew me to this book was the Foreword by Chris Brogan ... figuring that if it was good enough to get his "stamp of approval" at that level, it was probably something that I should check out. A couple of months back, I was scanning through said wish list and noticed that a "like new" copy had slipped down to 1¢ in the used channels, meaning that I could get it for $4 with shipping ...SOLD!

Now, the Social Media world moves *very* fast, and I'm sure that this would have been one of my go-to books when it came out in 2010 ... but this is *painfully* dated in 2014. I did not notice, until *after* I finished reading this, that there had been a new edition released in 2013 ... which would likely be much more up-to-date, and explains why this edition (heck, my copy was even author-signed!) had dropped to a penny.

That said (plus one other caveat that I'll address later), I really enjoyed this book ... I even liked its rather unusual format of rounded borders and out-of-the-lines graphic inserts and text boxes which work quite well here. However, section-by-section, it's hard to not react to the dated material, thus making this a difficult book to do a fair review of. Of course, in a book like this by a competent author/practitioner as Kabani, one can't help but have "evergreen" material to anchor one's focus, and she starts off with a definition:

> What is online marketing? Online marketing is the art and science (dare I say the Zen?) of leveraging the internet to get your message across so that you can move people to take action.

To activate this, she presents a "framework", using the acronym "ACT" to define three components of online marketing: Attract, Convert, and Transform. You attract the random stranger, convert them into a consumer (of your information), further convert them into a customer (by making a sale), by then involving the customer in your brand, you transform them into a tool for further attraction.

Now, this model gets a bit convoluted, but I'll try to just hit the high points here ... in the "attract" phase, "you need a great BOD" - Brand, Outcome, and Differentiator. You need to have a Brand identity that could ideally be summed up in one word. You need to define the Outcome that you're helping your customers achieve. And, you need to have something that makes you stand out in your niche, a Differentiator.

In the "convert" phase you take strangers and make them consumers, and (hopefully) take consumers and make them customers.

> *People become consumers when they subscribe to your blog, get on your newsletter list, or merely join your Facebook group ... They are <u>consuming</u> your information. At this point they have converted. They are no longer strangers. ...*
>
> *Offering people a sample of your work – whether through written content, pictures, or videos – can also lead them to buy from you.*
>
> *Ideally, the formula works like this:*
>
> *Consumption of Valuable Content + Time = Client (Customer)*

She next asks the question "What's the Best Conversion Tool?", and you can tell this was written before Facebook took over the whole online universe, as she is solidly suggesting one's own website. Of course, in the years since this was written a whole lot of people simply shifted over to Facebook pages, only to find that they weren't able to reach anybody unless they paid the piper. Obviously, the advice here is SOLID, just oddly anachronistic ... she notes: *"Remember, social media is not a selling tool! It is an attracting tool."*

In the "transform" phase she has two points: *"1. You have to do a good job."* and *"2. You have to <u>use</u> your success to attract more success."* ... with the further note that social media is an excellent vehicle for sharing stories, which establish your expertise with "social proof" that then helps to attract more prospects.

The next chapter deals with web sites, blogs, and SEO ... but, again, in 2010 contexts ... some of this is "basic" but other bits are not so "now" ... I'm sure this part of the book got updated in last year's edition. In this she also introduces another acronym – EMS – which is what your website needs to do: Educate, Market, and Sell. This then leads into a chapter on Social Media Marketing, which is fairly basic (bullet point: "Respect Other People Online" ... ya *think* so?), before launching into a look (one chapter each) at the three main platforms she recommends: Facebook, Twitter, and LinkedIn. To give you a taste of how "vintage" some of the info is here, the chapter head for Facebook notes its "300 Million" users ... compared to today's 1.32 *billion* users. So much has changed on each of these platforms, that it was cringe-worthy most of the way through those chapters ... obviously this was something that would have been updated in the new edition – but it's hard to keep up with moving targets like those. Same thing for the chapter following, on on-line video ... solid core ideas, long eclipsed info on hardware, software, and services.

OK ... up top I mentioned another caveat about this book that I'd get to later ... I guess this is as good a place as any. In various points in the book, the author promises that there's going to be constantly updated information on the book's website. In fact, she refers to the web site as a "living version" of the book *"with continuously updated content, video extras, MP3s, and more"*. However, when you go to the specified URL there is NONE of that there ... just a promo for the third edition of the book and various of the author's other services. If this was a "promise" made 10-15 years ago about maintaining a site, that would be one thing ... but this edition came out 4.5 years ago. Sure, I got this used for a penny plus shipping ... but I felt *abused* by not having updates on the promised web site. Maybe her publisher nixed "giving it away", but so quickly abandoning that promise is sort of a contrary thing for a social media guru to be doing.

Anyway ... next comes a very useful chapter on "Creating a Social Media Policy for Your Organization", which focuses on a 10-point plan for making sure you don't get in trouble with social media, your staff knows what they can and can't do, and how things will play out if situations do go wrong. A final chapter on tools (again, somewhat dated) follows, which closes with three points about setting this stuff in motion: *1. Strategize first. 2. Be human. 3. Have patience.* (with details on each ... good over-all advice). The book closes out with a chapter of Q&A (of variable usefulness), and 11 "case studies" featuring companies and organizations that are a very odd collection, which makes me assume they're "friends and clients" of Kabani's.

The Zen of Social Media Marketing[3] would have no doubt been one of my favorite books on the subject back in 2010, had I encountered it then, and perhaps the Third Edition is as useful now as this would have been at that time, but a mere 4 years down the road, this is very dated, and the broken promise of the no-longer "living version" on the web leaves a very unpleasant impression. I'll just leave it at that.

Notes:

1. http://btripp-books.livejournal.com/160557.html

2-3. http://amzn.to/1ylBnBK

Monday, October 27, 2014[1]

# And if they're Northern ...

OK ... this one came my way through a somewhat convoluted path. My elder daughter, who is in her first year at college, is having a problem with insomnia, and I went a-Googling to see what I might come up with to suggest to her. Among the resources I found was a book, *Say Good Night To Insomnia* by a Dr. Gregg Jacobs ... the name was familiar, and I did a bit of more research, and found out that the author was, indeed, an old college chum of mine from back when dinosaurs roamed the frozen tundra of Appleton, WI. While poking around in those corners of the web, I also noticed that he had written another book: The Ancestral Mind: Reclaim the Power[2] which sounded *very* interesting, and, while apparently out of print at the moment, was available from the on-line big boys' aftermarket sellers ... so I ordered a copy, which jumped right into my reading rotation.

Now, I'm not talking "out of school" here (as Gregg mentions most of this in the book), but the author was a bit of a strange bird (to all L.U. alums ... I know, "I should talk"), who spent every Friday night during football season off somewhere (I'm pretty sure it wasn't on campus) floating in a sensory deprivation tank, mentally going over his on-field routine (he was the placekicker, and ended up holding some conference records). He also managed to have co-authored a research paper on sensory deprivation tank therapy while an undergrad, which apparently is still referenced in the field, and pretty much launched him on his career path - he's currently assistant professor of psychiatry at Harvard Medical School and a Senior research scientist with the Mind/Body Institute of Harvard Medical School (not bad for a liberal arts college grad). All of this happening *before* stuff like the *Altered States* movie came out – so it was "pretty mysterious" at the time!

Anyway, the concept of the "ancestral mind" hooked me ... and he does a pretty good job of presenting arguments for paying more attention to the older parts of the brain, and their perceptual patterns. However, I don't think he makes a solid case for there being an "ancestral mind" per se ... early on he defines the Thinking Mind (henceforth TM) and the Ancestral Mind (AM) and treats them almost like they were two balls in a box ... and I'm still not fully convinced that they're that easily dividable.

Jacobs digs back in time and suggests that language developed some 35,000 years ago, and this was the spark for the evolution of the "Thinking Mind":

> *Language is an essential medium for all the activities we associate with the TM:*
> - *conscious awareness and reflection*
> - *analytical and abstract reasoning*

- *planning, anticipating, and predicting the future*
- *problem-solving and skill learning*

This was also, supposedly, the start of the sense of the individual, separated from nature, which *observed* the world, rather than *participate* in it the way the species had for vast stretches of time prior. Aside from the obvious utility of the items on the list above, how did the Thinking Mind get the upper hand over the Ancestral Mind? It simply *would not shut up*, "engaging in an almost continuous internal monologue" that anybody who has ever attempted sitting meditation will recognize. Jacobs then goes into a litany of the stressors of modern life, and how the Thinking Mind has driven these, especially with the concept of measured time … nothing comes "in its season", but "on a schedule", and the TM is constantly "keeping score" from how well you performed at work to how your car compares with the neighbors'.

Next we get into the "meat" part of the equation … where we might find the "Ancestral Mind" … he first posits a three-level functional division between the "reptilian brain", the "mammal brain", and the neocortex (where, of course the TM hangs out). The parts he points to for finding the AM are: the reticular formation (basic alertness), the thalamus (in charge of "directing traffic"), the amygdala (which "sets off alarms"), the hypothalamus (which "spreads the alarm" throughout the body), and all these working somewhat at counter-purposes to the prefrontal cortex (where thought and emotion meet and likely produce the "troublesome internal monologue"). The problem here is that the *hardware* evolved to deal with infrequent, but serious stress – avoid the saber-toothed tiger, not freak out that you can't afford the latest Apple accessory – and the TM has hijacked these systems to flood the body with signals that we're about to be lunch …for an endless stream of small issues of modern life.

All this theorizing aside, The Ancestral Mind[3] is essentially a "self-help book" for those of us who are over-stressed (frankly, every example of a modern-day TM-driven psychology "fail" Jacobs comes up with here was flashing neon as being something I deal with on a daily basis), and trying to get to a better place.

> *The TM's mental chatter shifts continually from the past to the future, from hopes to fears, running through endless arguments and schemes. Through the TM's internal monologue, we mull over our needs and desires, create mental lists of what we have to do, or what we regret we haven't accomplished. We endlessly review our worries and concerns, compounding and intensifying them while creating an exaggerated sense of time pressure to complete the tasks that face us.*

To fight this, Jacobs walks the readers through some tools, such as *cognitive restructuring* which is focused on stopping NAT's (negative automatic thoughts) before they take hold on the mind. One tool is to keep a "Cognitive Restructuring Diary", which has four columns, "Situation", "Emotion", "NAT", and "Reframed Thought" with a list of 10 questions to help diffuse the NATs (such as "4. Is there anything that might be positive about this situation?"). A second method of changing those negatives is the "double standard" technique ... in the sense that you're holding yourself to a far lower standard of reality that you might for others, asking the question *"Would I say this to a close friend with a similar problem?"*. Yet a third approach is suggested, tapping the emotional wisdom in "millions of years of evolution" contained in the AM, in this case asking *"Has anything like this happened to me in the past, and, if so, how did it turn out?"*. Once you get practice on these reframing approaches, he suggests a further tool, the "Stop – Breathe – Reframe" technique, where you recognize a stress situation that is likely to generate NATs, and say to yourself "STOP", then take a deep breath, and then reframe before the NATs get traction.

Now, folks who know me outside the on-line world realize that I'm a just a few gamma rays short of being Hulk on the "rage beast" scale, and another useful thing in here are 11 exercises for reducing anger. I could probably work a lot with #5: *"Don't expect perfection. Be realistic and modify your expectations for the behavior of those around you."*. There's also a list of "Rx's" here for using laughter to defuse stress ... his first question in this section is "How often do you laugh?", and I have to admit, the way my life's been going, that's probably down to once or twice *a month*, so I should probably pay more attention to these than I'd do "voluntarily". He also has a section on "faith" in here, but I'm not going to "go there". The chapter following is about social support, but this is another big set of triggers for the "moody loner" set, trust me on that.

One of the things that gets a lot of pages here is sleep ... with interesting research about how our "natural" sleep patterns – "polyphasic sleep" here – were pretty much wiped out with the invention of reliable lighting and the clock. Now, having been a guy who's "made do" with 4-5 hours of sleep a night nearly my entire adult life, I have a hard time taking seriously suggestions that dusk-to-dawn sleeping is a possibility. One of the things featured here, in relation to this is the "Relaxation Response" (RR), which is very much like classic hypnotic inductions, but (as far as I can recall), this material is *never* noted so. Like meditation, the RR is recommended as a "daily practice", if just for 10-20 minutes ... although he also charts out a "mini" less-than-a-minute version that can be done any time. Gregg really hits the target (for me) when he writes (emphasis mine):

> *The most difficult part of establishing regular RR practice is finding the time to do so. The tyranny of the Thinking Mind tells you that the day is too busy for relaxation, and will try to make you feel guilty or "unproductive". Think of the RR as something that will improve not just your mood and your health but your performance as well. It is something that you need and deserve. If you still can't find time for the*

> *RR, you are probably one of those who need it most*

The final chapters deal with how the TM is verbal, and the AM is visual, how the AM needs three things daily: music, light, and exercise, how times of solitude are renewing, and, finally, how we can look at pre-verbal children for a model of how the AM looks in practice (OK, maybe without smearing the veggies on the wall). Three appendices follow, one on (more) brain physiology, one on stress and health, and one on additional ~~hypnotic inductions~~ relaxation scripts.

Again, the parts I had issues with in The Ancestral Mind[4] were largely ones pointing directly to my *personal* issues with stress, etc., and I found the book fascinating, well researched, and very restrained for its genre. I'm still not sure I'd recognize the Ancestral Mind if I saw it, but I'll give Jacobs the credit that he's at least used the concept as a functional model for an "escape from (the worst elements of) modernity". As noted, this appears to be out of print, but the new/used guys at the online big boys' sites have "very good" copies of the hardcover for 1¢ (plus $3.99 shipping), so you don't have any real good excuses to not get yourself one if the above sounds interesting to you!

Notes:

1. http://btripp-books.livejournal.com/160930.html

2-4. http://amzn.to/1u9MgoP

Tuesday, October 28, 2014[1]

## Spontaneous, creative ...

I was very pleased to see Bellevue Literary Press' continuing participating in the LibraryThing.com "Early Reviewers" program, with Jonathan D. Moreno's new Impromptu Man: J.L. Moreno and the Origins of Psychodrama, Encounter Culture, and the Social Network[2] ... I had, in a previous "batch" hoped to have been matched (by the LTER "Almighty Algorithm") with his previous "Mind Wars", but hadn't at the time, and I was *thrilled* when the earlier book arrived along with this release ... I don't know if this was a bit of serendipity, or if the folks at BLP had paid attention on who had requested what books when, and seen that I'd been interested in getting that, but I'll give them the credit for being amazing.

Moreno is described as *the most interesting bioethicist of our time* (which, frankly, has the vibe of being "the most interestingly drying paint brand"), but "bioethics" doesn't enter into the equation here. This, instead, is a remarkable book, a rare case of a son getting to tell his father's story, with eloquence and understanding, and, naturally enough, compassion. For every child of a remarkable parent, this is the model of what a book honoring that life might be.

While Jonathan D. Moreno did have a chance to know his father, Jacob Levy Moreno, it was not a long relationship. The younger Moreno was born when the senior was in his 60's, with most of his pioneering work behind him, and his father died when the author was in his early 20's. Needless to say, that's a big shadow to deal with, and this book is very much exactly the younger Moreno doing that. One odd thing here is that the father is referred to by his initials J.L. throughout the book ... an avoidance of having to use "dad", "my father", or generating confusion with "Dr. Moreno" that I am quite familiar with (having spent the first fifteen years of my career working for my mother, who became M.T. pretty universally).

Who *is* J.L. Moreno? He is the doctor/showman who developed "Psychodrama", popularized group therapy, and created the science of "sociometry", whose relationship mapping via "sociograms" were the forerunners of social network analysis – the theoretical underpinnings of the platforms that have exploded across the world as social media. Big stuff ... and I wondered why I'd never heard of *him*. As I read through this, that question gained substance, because "J.L." was a tireless self-promoter and was famous in his day.

His biography is fascinating, having been born in Romania, his family moved to Vienna when he was a child, and he grew up amid the decline of the Hapsburg Empire. He attended the University of Vienna, and in 1917 became a Doctor of Medicine. He rejected Freud (having attended the elder psychologist's lectures), and began to both develop his theories for group therapy, and theatrically-based work. The culture of Vienna was amazing at this time, with Moreno attending lectures by Albert Einstein, and rubbing elbows in the cafes with famed psychiatrists, philosophers, composers, writers, and actors (and having an encounter in a park with a "disheveled postcard painter", Adolf Hitler). Moreno was trying to develop a theatrical model of "spontaneity" where actors were given, for instance, the basic details of a story in the day's papers, and expected to perform ... the broad strokes of which eventually took root and became what we currently call improv. His efforts, however, were not getting traction in Vienna, and in 1925 he had an opportunity to move to New York.

Needless to say, given the history of the time, this move (spurred by an involvement in a radio recording device on which he held the Austrian patent) was quite fortuitous, and even though it was difficult getting established in the U.S., it did mean that he avoided becoming either a victim of or refugee from the Nazis, as so many of his associates did in the following decades. Even after getting his medical license in 1927, it took what the author describes as "a marriage of convenience" to establish his citizenship. A rather charming term that Moreno came up with is *"surplus reality"* (generally "making stuff up"), and this came into play in this case, as Moreno claimed that his wife, Beatrice Beecher, died soon after their divorce (in the 30's), but state records indicate that she survived until 1972.

Once established, it took some time for Moreno to "pick up where he left off" in Europe. He had his book *The Theater of Spontaneity* translated to English, but had difficulty finding a publisher – eventually having it come out via Beacon House, a press that he established to publish his books and journals. Initially, Moreno was surviving seeing individual patients, but eventually worked his connections to be able to present programs at companies (such as Macy's) where he would put employees through "spontaneity tests", and returned to the theater with a "Living Newspaper" program, and eventually established his Impromptu Theater in 1931 and Group Theater soon after. Although these never reached the audience (or critical response) he had hoped for, they did seed other projects whose models are still very much with us.

While Moreno's theatrical ambitions were stalling, his psychiatric influence was growing. At the time, "mental health" was largely a warehousing issue ... people determined to be inconvenient to the society were shunted off to asylums, and it was in these contexts that Moreno did most of his work. One of his most enduring (from what has grown out of it) concepts was the "sociodynamic effect" (which is expressed in the variance from randomness in the "choices people make about with whom to associate" in any given community), which came to be visualized in "sociograms". Oddly, this seems to have started with observing the interactions of groups of *infants* at Mt. Sinai Hospital in New York City. Diagramming these interactions was a major breakthrough (albeit a challenging one in the pre-computer age), and the use of this method expanded from hospitals to schools, to asylums, to prisons, and eventually into various organizations – governmental and corporate.

One of the things which arose from his prison work was "group psychotherapy" - a term that he claimed to have coined in the early 30's – which also drew on other sources (Freud had written of Group Psychology in 1922), and eventually collided with the "therapeutic community" movement (the most famed example of which is Alcoholics Anonymous), further blurring Moreno's influence. In 1936 he was able to establish his own institute (initially "sanitarium") in Beacon, NY, where he was able to explore his theories of psychodrama, etc. for the next 30 years.

In WW2, Moreno was tapped to help develop assessment tools for the military. It appears that he was primarily working with the British OSS (based on sorting for "leadership"), although many of his associates began using his assorted methodologies with the U.S. Military. Following the war, several of these approaches were quickly implemented by the corporate world, although, again, Moreno's role in developing the ground of these was generally lost in the shuffle.

In the 60's, Moreno's concepts spread far and wide, with his concepts of "encounter", etc., cropping up in organizations such as Esalen, EST, Synanon, movements such as Transactional Analysis, and others, while his theatrical work inspired hundreds of new experimental theater groups. Towards the end of Impromptu Man[3], the author pulls in a long litany of things his father had influenced, and writes of following up with various associates that Moreno had worked with.

This is a fascinating look at a man, who in his time was "larger than life", but has been largely forgotten in the popular memory ... perhaps his son's book will help change that. This just came out this month, so you will likely be able to find it in the better-stocked remaining "brick and mortar" book vendors, but (of course) the on-line big boys have it (currently at a 22% discount). Just as Moreno's influence exhibits itself across a number of areas, this would be interesting to many different types of readers.

Notes:

1. http://btripp-books.livejournal.com/161230.html

2-3. http://amzn.to/1DKSsGO

Saturday, November 15, 2014[1]

# Lives in "interesting times" ...

It's been a *very* long time since I've read much of any fiction ... and especially "popular" fiction (as opposed to "classics" which are nominally fiction, but are filling holes in my over-all English Major reading list), but that "fluff" element in my to-be-read piles has migrated to the memoir. I was at the dollar store last month and found a nice hard-cover "deckle edge" edition of Susan Conley's The Foremost Good Fortune[2] on the shelf, and was amazed to find the copy that I picked up was even *signed by the author* (not to shabby for a buck!). This was a record of the author's time in China, having moved there with her husband and two small sons, right in the lead-up to the Beijing Olympics. They were relocating for her husband's job, a 2.5 year posting, and she was being uprooted from the writing workshop, literary magazine, and college seminars she'd been running back in Maine.

This would have been "interesting enough" in a fish-out-of-water sort of way, documenting all the strange new things she'd be encountering in China, but in the middle of their time in Beijing, she gets breast cancer ... lending a certain pathos to the tale, and bringing in factors that would have been unlikely to have featured otherwise.

As noted above, memoirs are much like fiction, as they're stories, and unfold as the book moves on ... which ends up with my not getting a lot of my little bookmarks in there (unless there are particularly gripping and/or informative things that I feel like I'll need to revisit), and I have to admit that in this case I had *none* ... which puts me at a disadvantage for the review.

The main take-away that I had from the book was that it was a particular window into the world of modern China that isn't something that I'd typically run across. There is a substantial, and varied, international community in Beijing, with representatives from every sort of company over there to set up businesses with the Chinese. Interestingly, this seems to be largely diverse, at least in Conley's experience, as she's not hanging out with Americans, but with Europeans, and assorted Asians for the most part.

One of the key elements that is a concern there is finding a nanny to work with the kids. The author has only the most rudimentary grasp of Chinese (although she hires a tutor), and having a local helps a lot for the shopping, and communications, etc. It seems that there is enough demand for these roles that it's slim pickings, and her tales of trying to find a good match (which never ends up as "ideal") are somewhat painful.

Her descriptions of the vast high-rise "luxury apartment" complexes which have been built all over the capital (and other major commercial centers) is fascinating ... with it being almost familiar yet very alien still. These are cheek-to-jowl with old market areas, and she could look out her windows and see a whole different world, almost a different age.

When she first discovers the cancer, she's largely at the mercy of a less-than-state-of-the-art medical establishment. A lot of the medical infrastructure is still based on Chinese traditional medicine, and this was not what she was wanting at that juncture. As things evolved, she made a number of trips back to the U.S. to have tests, and eventually surgery, done.

One of the sub-themes here is the author dealing with the psychological impact of having cancer, and the effect it was having on her two young sons. It's interesting to observe the interactions within the family, and wonder how that would have been different had that unfolded back in Maine, without the over-lay of life as a foreigner in China.

Of course, with a memoir (as opposed to a novel), one is looking at a slice of time in somebody's life ... and in this case it leads to a lot of stuff simply not getting "tidied up" within the narrative. I would have liked to have more "backstory" on both her and her husband's work (frankly, I can't recall what exactly his business *was* that had brought them to Beijing ... and his "character" was far less developed in the book than many others), to put a bit more context on how they're reacting to the various things they encounter. And, when they move back home, the story's pretty much over ... naturally enough, she's writing from the midst of living her life, so can't bring things to any particular conclusion.

In the course of the story, they go on a number of road trips (they have a driver, who becomes somewhat part of the family), which allow Conley to describe many fascinating countryside vignettes, some quite striking in their differences from the "modern" lifestyle in the city. Of course, life in the city isn't always that modern ... there is one bit where a homing pigeon had stunned itself hitting their windows, and their nanny/cook was *very* interested in getting a hold of the "plump" bird ... no doubt with recipes in mind!

Again, The Foremost Good Fortune[3] was an interesting read, primarily due to its look into a world that I'd have no other exposure to ... personally, I probably would have *liked* the book more if it was focused on the expat experience in Beijing and China in general, but the cancer story, and the whole dynamic of dealing with small children in that environment, are probably more its *raison d'être*.

As I've often noted, it surprises me to find books that are in the dollar stores still in the major channels, but this is still being offered at nearly full price by the on-line big boys, and, having only come out in 2011, it might still be available in the brick-and-mortar stores. However, being in the dollar store channel, it's available for a penny (plus shipping) via the new/used vendors. This is certainly not something that I would have even considered "at retail", but it's an agreeable read for a buck.

Notes:

1. http://btripp-books.livejournal.com/161516.html

2-3. http://amzn.to/1C88gRM

Sunday, November 16, 2014[1]

# The ABCs of early Godin ...

As regular readers of this space will recognize, I've read (and reviewed) a *lot* of books by Seth Godin ... I think I'm up to 10 at this point. Some of these have been new-ish, and some of these have been embarrassingly dated, some I've raved about and some have been just OK. This one is in the middle somewhere, I think. First of all, I wonder if there was *intentional* irony involved with giving Small Is the New Big: and 183 Other Riffs, Rants, and Remarkable Business Ideas[2] its title ... as at over 300 pages, it's certainly one of Godin's *bigger* books. This does suffer from one aspect of its vintage – the link for looking up the dates of the initial publication of the component pieces has gone bad in the absorption of Squidoo into HubPages ... and I couldn't find the info on the latter site. The reason I went digging for that is that I was wanting to toss around dates here, but couldn't, but the publication date was 2006.

This is a factor in discussing the book, as it is a collection of *"eight years of {Godin's} very best blog posts, magazine columns, and e-books"* ... 184 pieces, judging from the subtitle. Obviously, things written 8 years prior to 2006 pushes the envelope for being pertinent to current realities (going back as much as 16 years ago) ... and that info is *not* included here – just referred to on a site which seems to no longer have the info. Now, if this was *chronologically* arranged, one could get a sense of the age of the materials, but it's not ... nor is it "curated" into thematic blocks ... no, the book is organized *alphabetically by title*, creating quite a heterogeneous arrangement of topics!

Of course, this leads me to the observation that this is a VERY difficult book to generate a coherent review of ... it is, after all, the print equivalent of reading his blog from 1998-2006, in an order which allows for no "theme", other than those which are endemic to Godin's subject matter, and no way to specifically filter for what's a "vintage" statement or what might be being used "ironically" (for example, in 2014 stories of movie rental chains tend towards reading like the latter, even if they were penned sufficiently long ago that they are actually the former).

My first thought in reflecting back on Small Is The New Big[3] was that it could make a very nice introduction to Seth Godin for folks who were unfamiliar with his writings. However, I'm hesitant to promote it in that frame, as the unpredictable age of individual pieces would, for somebody not familiar with Godin, possibly lead to a rejection of his perceptions due to the "old news" aspect which *does* creep in here every now and again (as one would expect simply from it being a book released *8 years ago*, let alone being a collection of materials from 8 years prior to that). Fortunately, much of what's in here is "evergreen", and reflects key elements of Godin's on-going marketing message, but it's certainly not "new" or "fresh" like his The Icarus Deception[4] or other recent releases.

Of course, Godin being Godin, there are lots of choice bits in here ... and I marked a few to share with you. In the "Fifty States, Flamethrowers, and Sticky Traditions" piece, he throws a light on something I'd not considered previously (illustrating how the "status quo" often gets established somewhat randomly):

> More than a hundred years ago, Kaiser Wilhelm wanted to get rid of his enemies in the German government. He noticed that they were all over sixty-five years old. So he decreed that this was the official retirement age, and it still is.

Pretty amazing, yes? In the same section he talks about how other "bad ideas stick around forever". Speaking of bad ideas, he delves deeper into this in the "Pigeons, Superstitious" piece, which starts with how pigeons will connect what they were doing when food first arrived in a particular situation, and keep doing that thing (head bobbing, etc.), and ends up looking at religious (and other) fundamentalists:

> These people are characterized, I believe, by two traits. First, they live according to a large body of superstitions. Second, they believe that they are right and everybody else is wrong. They believe that they have found the one and only truth, and they can't abide changing old rules in light of new data. <u>Fundamentalists decide whether they can accept a new piece of information based on how it will affect their prior belief system, not based on whether it is actually true.</u>
> ...
> When I meet someone who's willing to disregard an obvious truth just because it conflicts with his worldview, I wonder about his judgment. I wonder what other truths he's willing to ignore in order to preserve his superstitions. When such a person is in charge, I do more than worry. I think that we're obligated to start pointing out superstitions at work, in politics – anywhere we find them. Superstitions are the final vestiges of prescientific humankind, and they make the workplace (and the world) a scary one.

Now, some of these are less "heavy" ... like the "Polka button" that he reports being next to an escalator in a Milwaukee conference facility ... push the button and hear polka music during your ride! He points out various bits and pieces, like: *"1. Humans tend to work on a problem until they get a good-enough solutions, not a solution that's right. 2. The marketplace often* rewards solutions that are cheaper and good enough, instead of investing in the solution that promises to lead to the right answer." ... I wonder how old this one is, as it sort of goes counter to the "ship now" philosophy where the "minimal viable product" is pushed out before finding the "right" final version.

In the section "Trust and Respect, Courage and Leadership", Godin complains about how respect for the consumer has suffered of late:

> Somewhere along the way, marketers stopped acting like real people. We substituted a new set of ethics, one built around "buyer beware" and the letter of the law. Marketers, in order to succeed in a competitive marketplace, decided to see what they could get away with instead of what they could deliver.
>
> ...
>
> The magic kicks in when marketers are smart enough and brave enough to combine trust with respect. When a marketer doesn't frisk you on the way out of a retail establishment, or trusts you to make intelligent decisions, you remember it. The number of companies that keep their promises and respect their customers' intelligence, alas, is quite tiny.

Interestingly, Godin appears to have come out with a "new" version of this – a book which collects a similar batch of writings from 2006-2012 (where he must have been a lot more prolific – it runs twice the length of this volume!), *Whatcha Gonna Do with That Duck?* (which I've not picked up as yet).

Small Is the New Big[5] is still in print, with the on-line big boys still having it at a standard discount, so it might well still be out in your neighborhood brick-and-mortar book vendor. Of course, having been out as long as it has, copies have worked their way down through the used channels, and you can get a "very good" copy for as little as 1¢ (plus $3.99 shipping, of course), which is how I came by *my* copy. If you like Seth Godin, you'll like this book, but it's not likely to be providing any massive "aha!" moments ... it will be a pleasant read, however, with fascinating bits all through.

Notes:

1. http://btripp-books.livejournal.com/161767.html
2-3. http://amzn.to/1IJ3OLr
4. http://btripp-books.livejournal.com/155932.html
5. http://amzn.to/1IJ3OLr

Saturday, December 6, 2014[1]

# Bleh ...

So ... the downside of getting books from the Library-Thing.com "Early Reviewers" program is that sometimes the book that the Almighty Algorithm matches to one's library is a *clunker*, and this has happened to me every now and again. Of course, being the OCD beastie that I am, I'm pretty much incapable of saying "man, this *sucks* and I'm not going to read another word", since I've agreed (as part of the LTER program) to read the book and write a review thereof. So I read the book ... and here I am to report on same.

The good news is that Aingeal Rose O'Grady's The Nature of Reality: Akashic Guidance for Understanding Life and Its Purpose[2] wasn't as uniformly horrid as it started out. This appears (from the cover, etc.) to be "Book 2" of the "Honest-to-God Series" that the author and her publishers are putting out. There is only passing mention of the previous book here, but I'm suspecting that a lot of the set-up for her "method" and world-view were covered there and that they're just *assuming* that readers of this are on-board with all that. Heck, they spend two pages in the front material "explaining" a chalk illustration on the back cover ... you'd think they'd explain what's going on in the book before dropping the reader neck deep in the sewage.

The format of the book is a series of questions that the author answers, based on "information" that she's getting from "The Source" (oh, what a more *fun* book this would be if that was "The Source" from the old Charmed TV show!). One wonders if the author had "been dropped on her head when she was very small" or the like, as she "communicates" with The Source via patterns of light ... which she then translates into words ... which certainly sounds like "auguries via synesthesia" - communicating the intents of the universe by interpreting the stuff she's seeing! Another irritating thing is that they never really explain who is asking the questions ... at one point it sounds like they're being passed along to her via her life partner (who, exasperatingly, is referred to as a six-letter acronym), but it also seems like they're coming from an audience (of total doofuses) who are desperately clutching each to their own "newage" delusions, and are looking for O'Grady to bolster their beliefs (to her credit, she occasionally does shoot down particularly loony drivel).

Here's the crux of what made the book nearly unreadable to me ... so much "newage sewage" and so little supportable *theory* (I'm not even asking for defensible statements, just something that at least *appears* to hold together as a coherent model!). I would have much preferred it if the author would tell her SFB questioners to shut the hell up, and start laying out a system of "color pattern interpretation" that would say *"when you get these, it means that this sort of thing is coming through, and if they're this shade it indicates*

X, Y, or Z". I came close to giving up on the book in Chapter 2, because it is all about DNA ... and, evidently various woo-woo newage scams that latch onto the concept of the molecule and offer DNA-based (I've never hit a clearer case for dragging out the classic line from Inigo Montoya in *The Princess Bride*: **"You keep using that word. I do not think it means what you think it means."**) "services" such as *"22-strand activation through the use of crystals"* and similar snake oil ... to "The Source's" credit it says that's not possible – but one gets the vibe that O'Grady is in on that twaddle, or she would have simply bitch-slapped the loonies who asked: *"How similar is the DNA of humans to Sasquatch and Mermaids?"* (where does she *find* this level of delusional moron?) rather than spinning out an actual answer!

The one saving grace here is that, on *some* subjects, she actually ventures into presenting something of a system. One was Angels ... which had structure and a reasonable level of consistency (despite including asinine queries about the *gender* of audience members' favorites angels) ... and the other was her discussion of Time. In both of these cases she was at least coherent in taking "visions of light" and interpreting them as communications from "god" (the whole "god" question here is pretty blurry, of course, but not as wide-open as one might assume for something this deep down the newage rabbit hole).

Again, the whole book is Q&A ... organized in general topic areas ... but this means it swings in and out of what could be seen as "quality" and what is clearly idiotic blithering. For example, immediately preceding a question *"Do dream catchers really keep negative spirits out?"*, there is this *very* interesting bit:

> People who dream of disasters seem to like it when their dreams come true, which they view as proof that they are psychic, or that they can somehow predict events through their dreams. They don't realize that they may be helping to manifest those scenarios by giving them validity and energy. If you talk to people who continually dream of things that come true, you will find that most often they are dreaming of someone dying, or some disaster. These people may think that they are really psychic and able to tune into the future, but what is most likely really happening is that they are being used by dark forces to help manifest those probabilities. We need to remember how powerful our minds are. If we remember that every thought takes form on some level, we will be more conscious of what kinds of thoughts and visuals we are giving our energies and emotions to.

These are not the words of a fluff-bunny unicorn-rainbow-farts type ... so I'm really, really, hoping that there may be some core of reality in O'Grady's material – and that she's not simply Gurdjieffianly "shearing the sheep" with her descriptions of her internal light show!

Although this was a recent offering in the "Early Reviewer" program, The Nature of Reality[3] has been out over a year. I don't know what that means for its being available in the brick-and-mortar vendors of this sort of stuff, but it's oddly not dropped much in price over on the on-line sources, so if you (for some inexplicable reason) want to obtain a copy, you're going to have to shell out pretty close to the cover price. This is *not* a book that I would have "free range" picked up, or even finished reading … but I would be interested if Ms. O'Grady came out with a "serious" book analyzing her interface and communications with "The Source", as there do seem to be a few kernels of usable information deeply buried in the muck of this.

Notes:

1. http://btripp-books.livejournal.com/162003.html
2-3. http://amzn.to/1BclHBi

Sunday, December 7, 2014[1]

# This actually helped ...

As regular readers of this space (especially if you're reading it in my main blog) will recognize, depression is something that I've been dealing with for a long time, made more pointed as the years pile up with my not being able to find a full-time job (I'm up to *five and a half years* at this point). It's hard to get "up" when you're in free-fall *down*.

I'm not sure how Andrew Weil's Spontaneous Happiness[2] got on my radar, but I only ordered it a few weeks back (after it having been parked on my Amazon wish list for quite a while). Needless to say, getting books about "being happy" is a huge pivot for me (as anybody who's been exposed to my poetry[3] can no doubt attest), but things have been so bleak, I'll try nearly anything (although I haven't been able to bring myself to listening to "happy" music instead of my usual goth/metal mix). Needless to say, it was very encouraging to find that Dr. Weil has struggled with depression most of his life:

> *Over the years I tried various forms of psychotherapy and counseling but got little benefit from them. Once, in my early forties, I filled a prescription for an antidepressant but gave it up after a few days because I could not tolerate its side effects. It numbed my body and dulled my mind. ... Eventually I came to accept my depressive episodes as existential in nature – part of my being – to be endured and not inflicted on others. This way of thinking increased my tendency to be antisocial and isolated, traits not uncommon in writers.*

Like Weil, I tried a number of psychiatric drugs (in the wake of my publishing company failing in 2004), but could not tolerate any ... and eventually figured being an anguished *authentic* me was better than being a dulled, zombified, shadow of myself ... who just happened to not be feeling the pain of existence.

Weil points to a lot of data about how depression, and "being unhappy" more generally, may simply be a side effect of the modern lifestyle. Cases of depression have multiplied *ten times* since the end of WW2, and are highest in first-world urban settings (oh, like the downtown Chicago highrise I've lived in for the past 33 years). He notes:

> *Human beings evolved to thrive in natural environments and in bonded social groups. Few of us today can enjoy such a life and the emotional equilibrium it engenders, but out genetic predisposition for it has not changed.*

While there is quite a bit of his personal story in here, it's really not an autobiographical look at the author's struggles, but an attempt at a regimen for improving one's psychological state. The book features four chapters on "theory", three chapters on "practice", and a final chapter presenting "An 8-Week Program for Emotional Well-Being".

Of course, *"Brendan doesn't play well with the other children."* (funny how notes home from kindergarten never seem to fade), so the odds of my throwing myself into a lifestyle-disrupting 8-week program are slim to none from the get-go ... and much of the material in the book focuses forward to how it integrates into the "plan", which had me mentally fighting a lot as I read it.

There are parts here, however, that I was on board with predictably ... such as "Integrating Eastern and Western Psychology". It's no surprise that this is part of Weil's approach, as he's a major figure in the field of "Integrative Medicine" ... and he pulls in Native American elements, as well as Buddhist thought, from Gautama's teachings two and a half millennia ago, to projects pioneered by the Dalai Lama with psychological groups in our own era.

In the "Practice" section, the three chapters deal with "Caring for the Body", "Retraining and Caring for the Mind" and "Secular Spirituality and Emotional Well-Being". Weil goes into a lot of "CBT" (cognitive-behavioral therapy) work in the middle one of these, while contrasting it with classical psychotherapy and related approaches. In the latter, he defines his approach with:

> *I find it awkward for two reasons to discuss spirituality. First, many people confuse spirituality with religion. Although the two may overlap, religion usually demands dogmatic adherence to beliefs that are ultimately not provable, and differences in those beliefs are common causes of suspicion and conflict in our world. Second, spiritual reality concerns the nonphysical aspect of our being. Western science and medicine adhere to the philosophy of materialism, which dictates that only what can be directly perceived, touched, and measured is real; to materialists, the term <u>nonphysical reality</u> is an oxymoron.*

And, in this section, discusses "spiritual" approaches as divergent as interacting with pets, appreciating art, and practicing forgiveness.

However, the most significant element in the book (for me) is in the "Caring for the Body" section, where he discusses many ways to improve mood by way of exercise, limiting caffeine, and avoidance of various convenience foods (you see where this was heading in *my* lifestyle?) but in amid all those "ain't gonna happen" things there was the dietary supplement part ... and especially his suggestion of adding fish oil to one's diet:

> *Many studies link specific nutrient deficiencies to suboptimal brain function and mental/emotional*

> health. The most important by far is lack of omega-3 fatty acids. These special fats are critically important for both physical and and mental health. The body needs regular daily intake of adequate amounts of both EPA and DHA, two long-chain omega-3 fats that are abundant in oily fish from cold northern waters but otherwise are hard to come by. ... A great deal of scientific data links low tissue levels of EPA and DHA to a host of mental/emotional disorders, ... I recommend that everyone take 2 to 4 grams of a good fish oil product every day. ... Not only does it offer real protection against depression,<u>but I believe it can help move your emotional set point away from sadness and towards contentment.</u> {emphasis mine}

I finished reading this book less than two weeks ago, but started taking a fish oil supplement right away ... and I have been *amazed*. It's no psychological panacea, but the effect was quite notable. My "depression elevator" used to go down to the 25th, 50th, etc., sub-basement *deep* into "life is miserable, what is the point?" territory, but since adding fish oil to my daily handful of pills, that has a new "floor" never getting much lower than maybe the 5th to 10th sub-basement. Still no "happy camper", but far, far less dire and desperate! I would recommend Dr. Weil's recommendations on this to *anybody* struggling with depression.

As noted, the book culminates with "An 8-Week Program for Emotional Well-Being", which pulls together all the bits and pieces laid out in the preceding sections into an action plan ... that is way too involved for me, personally. Like the fish oil, I'm up for cherry-picking items that I can integrate into my day-to-day existence, but I'd probably need to check in to a retreat center (wouldn't it be nice if there were "happiness" rehab programs?) to be able to shift as many gears in my life to be able to attempt a regimen like he suggests here. I do realize, though, that there *are* folks out there who are happy to jump into this sort of thing, so that might be something that would appeal to you.

The book has several useful things at the end, with an appendix outlining Weil's "Anti-Inflammatory Diet", another with a listing of suggested books, web sites, and sources of supplies, and an oddly-formatted section of notes (which are related back to page numbers, but not the other way, so I guess one is supposed to keep an eye on that while reading through the text) which has some interesting contextual info.

Anyway, I certainly found Spontaneous Happiness[4] a very useful book, although not being the sort of thing that I could simply "jump into" ... but I'm guessing that others (who are more attuned to the "self-help" genre) might find this *quite* engaging. I would certainly recommend it to anybody who is struggling with depression. I'm surprised, frankly, that this has only been out for a few years, but has already worked its way down to being available for a penny for "very good" copies of the hardcover (and at the moment one of the Amazon's new/used vendors has a "like new" copy for a whopping 4¢), so you don't have much of a barrier to picking this up!

Notes:

1. http://btripp-books.livejournal.com/162217.html
2. http://amzn.to/15dOmIk
3. http://eschatonbooks.com/
4. http://amzn.to/15dOmIk

# QR code links to the on-line reviews:

Everyday Book Marketing:
Promotion ideas to fit your regularly scheduled life
by
Midge Raymond

Why the World Doesn't Seem to Make Sense:
An Inquiry into Science, Philosophy, and Perception
by
Steve Hagen

Egyptomania: Our Three Thousand Year
Obsession with the Land of the Pharaohs
by
Bob Brier

Highly Recommended: Harnessing the Power
of Word of Mouth and Social Media
to Build Your Brand and Your Business
by
Paul M. Rand

Quick and Nimble: Lessons from Leading CEOs on How to Create a Culture of Innovation
by
Adam Bryant

Maximize Your Social: A One-Stop Guide to Building a Social Media Strategy for Marketing and Business Success
by
Neal Schaffer

Essence of the Dhammapada: The Buddha's Call to Nirvana
by
Eknath Easwaran

Losing Our Religion: The Liberal Media's Attack on Christianity
by
S.E. Cupp

Present at the Creation: the Story of CERN
and the Large Hadron Collider
by
Amir D. Aczel

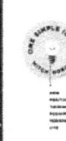

One Simple Idea:
How Positive Thinking Reshaped Modern Life
by
Mitch Horowitz

The Demon Under the Microscope: From Battlefield
Hospitals to Nazi Labs, One Doctor's Heroic Search
for the World's First Miracle Drug
by
Thomas Hager

The Freaks Shall Inherit the Earth: Entrepreneurship
for Weirdos, Misfits, and World Dominators
by
Chris Brogan

Spin Sucks: Communication and
Reputation Management in the Digital Age
by
Gini Dietrich

Biodiesel America: How to Achieve Energy Security,
Free America from Middle-east Oil Dependence
And Make Money Growing Fuel
by
Josh Tickell

How Excellent Companies Avoid Dumb Things:
Breaking the 8 Hidden Barriers
that Plague Even the Best Businesses
by
Neil Smith

The Icarus Deception: How High Will You Fly?
by
Seth Godin

Free Money "They" Don't Want You to Know About
by
Kevin Trudeau

Likeable Social Media: How to Delight Your Customers,
Create an Irresistible Brand, and Be Generally Amazing
on Facebook (& Other Social Networks)
by
Dave Kerpen

An Enemy of the People
by
Henrik Ibsen

The Pirates' ~~Code~~ Guidelines:
A Booke for Those Who Desire to Keep to the Code
and Live a Pirate's Life
by
Joshamee Gibbs

Creativity, Inc.: Overcoming the Unseen Forces
That Stand in the Way of True Inspiration
by
Ed Catmull

Conscious Millionaire:
Grow Your Business by Making a Difference
by
J.V. Crum, III

Before the First Shots Are Fired:
How America Can Win Or Lose Off The Battlefield
by
General Tony Zinni

The Conscious Universe:
The Scientific Truth of Psychic Phenomena
by
Dean Radin

Unleashing the Ideavirus: Stop Marketing AT People!
Turn Your Ideas into Epidemics by Helping
Your Customers Do the Marketing thing for You
by
Seth Godin

Startup Mixology: Tech Cocktail's Guide to Building,
Growing, and Celebrating Startup Success
by
Frank Gruber

The Fortune Cookie Chronicles:
Adventures in the World of Chinese Food
by
Jennifer 8. Lee

Shortcut: How Analogies Reveal Connections,
Spark Innovation, and Sell Our Greatest Ideas
by
John Pollack

Free: The Future of a Radical Price
by
Chris Anderson

The Social Employee: How Great Companies
Make Social Media Work
by
Cheryl & Mark Burgess

Riveted: The Science of Why Jokes Make Us Laugh,
Movies Make Us Cry, and Religion Makes Us
Feel One with the Universe
by
Jim Davies

Border Insecurity: Why Big Money, Fences,
and Drones Aren't Making Us Safer
by
Sylvia Longmire

UnSelling: The New Customer Experience
by
Scott Stratten

The Zen of Social Media Marketing: An Easier Way
to Build Credibility, Generate Buzz,
and Increase Revenue
by
Shama Hyder Kabani

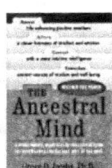
The Ancestral Mind: Reclaim the Power
by
Dr. Gregg Jacobs

Impromptu Man: J.L. Moreno and the Origins
of Psychodrama, Encounter Culture,
and the Social Network
by
Jonathan D. Moreno

The Foremost Good Fortune
by
Susan Conley

Small Is the New Big: and 183 Other Riffs, Rants,
and Remarkable Business Ideas
by
Seth Godin

The Nature of Reality: Akashic Guidance
for Understanding Life and Its Purpose
by
Aingeal Rose O'Grady

Spontaneous Happiness
by
Andrew Weil

# CONTENTS - ALPHABETICAL BY AUTHOR

| Author | Title | Page |
|---|---|---|
| Amir D. Aczel | Present at the Creation | 24 |
| Chris Anderson | Free | 83 |
| Bob Brier | Egyptomania | 7 |
| Chris Brogan | The Freaks Shall Inherit the Earth | 33 |
| Adam Bryant | Quick and Nimble | 13 |
| Mark Burgess | The Social Employee | 86 |
| Ed Catmull | Creativity, Inc. | 60 |
| Susan Conley | The Foremost Good Fortune | 109 |
| J.V. Crum, III | Conscious Millionaire | 63 |
| S.E. Cupp | Losing Our Religion | 21 |
| Jim Davies | Riveted | 90 |
| Gini Dietrich | Spin Sucks | 36 |
| Eknath Easwaran | Essence of the Dhammapada | 18 |
| Joshamee Gibbs | The Pirates' Code | 58 |
| Seth Godin | The Icarus Deception | 45 |

| | | | |
|---|---|---|---|
| Seth Godin | *Small Is the New Big* | page | 111 |
| Seth Godin | *Unleashing the Ideavirus* | page | 71 |
| Frank Gruber | *Startup Mixology* | page | 74 |
| Steve Hagen | *Why the World Doesn't Seem to Make Sense* | page | 4 |
| Thomas Hager | *The Demon Under the Microscope* | page | 30 |
| Mitch Horowitz | *One Simple Idea* | page | 27 |
| Henrik Ibsen | *An Enemy of the People* | page | 55 |
| Gregg Jacobs | *The Ancestral Mind* | page | 102 |
| Shama Kabani | *The Zen of Social Media Marketing* | page | 99 |
| Dave Kerpen | *Likeable Social Media* | page | 52 |
| Jennifer 8. Lee | *The Fortune Cookie Chronicles* | page | 77 |
| Sylvia Longmire | *Border Insecurity* | page | 93 |
| Jonathan D. Moreno | *Impromptu Man* | page | 106 |
| Aingeal Rose O'Grady | *The Nature of Reality* | page | 114 |
| John Pollack | *Shortcut* | page | 80 |
| Dean Radin | *The Conscious Universe* | page | 68 |

| | | |
|---|---|---|
| Paul M. Rand  *Highly Recommended* | page | 10 |
| Midge Raymond  *Everyday Book Marketing* | page | 1 |
| Neal Schaffer  *Maximize Your Social* | page | 16 |
| Neil Smith  *How Excellent Companies Avoid Dumb Things* | page | 42 |
| Scott Stratten & Alison Kramer  *UnSelling* | page | 96 |
| Josh Tickell  *Biodiesel America* | page | 39 |
| Kevin Trudeau  *Free Money "They" Don't Want You to Know About* | page | 49 |
| Andrew Weil  *Spontaneous Happiness* | page | 117 |
| General Tony Zinni &. Tony Koltz  *Before the First Shots Are Fired* | page | 65 |

# CONTENTS - ALPHABETICAL BY TITLE

|  |  |  |
|---|---|---|
| *The Ancestral Mind* <br> Gregg Jacobs | page | 102 |
| *Before the First Shots Are Fired* <br> General Tony Zinni &. Tony Koltz | page | 65 |
| *Biodiesel America* <br> Josh Tickell | page | 39 |
| *Border Insecurity* <br> Sylvia Longmire | page | 93 |
| *Conscious Millionaire* <br> J.V. Crum, III | page | 63 |
| *The Conscious Universe* <br> Dean Radin | page | 68 |
| *Creativity, Inc.* <br> Ed Catmull | page | 60 |
| *The Demon Under the Microscope* <br> Thomas Hager | page | 30 |
| *Egyptomania* <br> Bob Brier | page | 7 |
| *An Enemy of the People* <br> Henrik Ibsen | page | 55 |
| *Essence of the Dhammapada* <br> Eknath Easwaran | page | 18 |
| *Everyday Book Marketing* <br> Midge Raymond | page | 1 |
| *The Foremost Good Fortune* <br> Susan Conley | page | 109 |
| *The Fortune Cookie Chronicles* <br> Jennifer 8. Lee | page | 77 |
| *The Freaks Shall Inherit the Earth* <br> Chris Brogan | page | 33 |

| Title | Author | Page |
|---|---|---|
| *Free Money "They" Don't Want You to Know About* | Kevin Trudeau | 49 |
| *Free* | Chris Anderson | 83 |
| *Highly Recommended* | Paul M. Rand | 10 |
| *How Excellent Companies Avoid Dumb Things* | Neil Smith | 42 |
| *The Icarus Deception* | Seth Godin | 45 |
| *Impromptu Man* | Jonathan D. Moreno | 106 |
| *Likeable Social Media* | Dave Kerpen | 52 |
| *Losing Our Religion* | S.E. Cupp | 21 |
| *Maximize Your Social* | Neal Schaffer | 16 |
| *The Nature of Reality* | Aingeal Rose O'Grady | 114 |
| *One Simple Idea* | Mitch Horowitz | 27 |
| *The Pirates' Code* | Joshamee Gibbs | 58 |
| *Present at the Creation* | Amir D. Aczel | 24 |
| *Quick and Nimble* | Adam Bryant | 13 |
| *Riveted* | Jim Davies | 90 |
| *Shortcut* | John Pollack | 80 |

| | | | |
|---|---|---|---|
| Seth Godin | *Small Is the New Big* | page | 111 |
| Mark Burgess | *The Social Employee* | page | 86 |
| Gini Dietrich | *Spin Sucks* | page | 36 |
| Andrew Weil | *Spontaneous Happiness* | page | 117 |
| Frank Gruber | *Startup Mixology* | page | 74 |
| Seth Godin | *Unleashing the Ideavirus* | page | 71 |
| Scott Stratten & Alison Kramer | *UnSelling* | page | 96 |
| Steve Hagen | *Why the World Doesn't Seem to Make Sense* | page | 4 |
| Shama Kabani | *The Zen of Social Media Marketing* | page | 99 |

www.ingramcontent.com/pod-product-compliance
Lightning Source LLC
Chambersburg PA
CBHW070455100426
42743CB00010B/1631